.... the joy of ....

cider

All You Ever Wanted to Know About Drinking and Making Hard Cider

JEANETTE HURT

Skyhorse Publishing

Photos courtesy of Eden Specialty Ciders: pages 27, 28, 29, 56, 59, 63, 67 (top), 70, 81, 85, 87, 129, 130, 171, 172, 174
Photos courtesy of Hidden Cave Cidery: 107, 109, 111, 117, 120
Photos courtesy of Kyle Edwards: 16, 26
Photos courtesy of Ramborn Cider: 94, 98, 99
Photos courtesy of Tur Espana: xiii, 36, 89, 95, 96, 172, 176
Photos courtesy of Virtue Cider: v, vi, viii, x, xiv, 2, 3, 4, 9, 11, 12, 14, 15, 19, 21, 30, 31, 32, 33, 35, 39, 40, 42, 46, 48, 52, 54, 60, 62, 64, 66, 67 (bottom), 68, 69, 73, 76, 88, 90, 91, 92, 93, 104, 113, 125, 126, 137, 139, 143, 146, 147, 153, 156, 159, 161, 164, 166, 170, 178, 180, 187, 188

Skyhorse Publishing books may be purchased in bulk at special discounts for sales promotion, corporate gifts, fund-raising, or educational purposes. Special editions can also be created to specifications. For details, contact the Special Sales Department, Skyhorse Publishing, 307 West 36th Street, 11th Floor, New York, NY 10018 or info@skyhorsepublishing.com.

Skyhorse® and Skyhorse Publishing® are registered trademarks of Skyhorse Publishing, Inc.®, a Delaware corporation.

Visit our website at www.skyhorsepublishing.com.

10 9 8 7 6 5 4 3 2 1

Library of Congress Cataloging-in-Publication Data

Names: Hurt, Jeanette, author.
Title: The joy of cider : all you ever wanted to know about drinking and making hard cider / Jeanette Hurt.
Description: New York, NY : Skyhorse Publishing, [2019] | Includes index.
Identifiers: LCCN 2019012224 | ISBN 9781510742888 (pbk. : alk. paper)
Subjects: LCSH: Cider. | Apples. | LCGFT: Cookbooks.
Classification: LCC TP563 .H87 2019 | DDC 641.3/411--dc23 LC record available at https://lccn.loc.gov/2019012224

Cover design by Daniel Brount
Cover photos courtesy of Hidden Cave Cidery and Virtue Cider

Print ISBN: 978-1-5107-4288-8
Ebook ISBN: 978-1-5107-4289-5

Printed in China

This book is dedicated to my writing and journalism friends:
Damon Brown, Kristine Kierzek, Erin O'Donnell, Jennie
Tunkieicz, Paula Hermann, Susie Robarge, Erica Maley,
and the best agent an author could ever have, Marilyn Allen.

CONTENTS

Foreword

By Gregory Hall, founder of Virtue Cider

THREE FRIENDS WALK INTO A bar. One orders a beer, the next one a glass of wine, the third a cocktail.

What's the punchline in a cider book? Is it that they only think of cider as being the sweet stuff they get in the fall from the apple-picking farm? Or is it that the joke takes place back in 2010, "before cider?"

Because now is cider's time.

Why is it cider's time, in 2019? Well, dear friend, sit down and let me tell you.

Cider is simple. Cider is made from pressed apples. Period. End of sentence. Full stop. Raise your hand if you've heard of apples! That's what I thought. Take one step forward if you've ever picked an apple straight from a tree and taken a big, juicy bite. Now take a step back if you've ever picked fresh hops from the vine, distilled your own sour mash or done a malolactic fermentation. All three?! I'm so proud of you; both of you. So yes, cider is simple. Everyone understands apples.

Cider is local. Most of us have picked local apples. Maybe you had to get in a car for a bit, maybe you just walked out back. But 83 percent of Americans can drive to pick apples and be home for dinner. Local is hot—just check out the line at your local brewery (most don't use local barley or hops) or your local coffee roaster (ehh, umm, nevermind). But apples grow just about everywhere. In the age of provenance, cider wins again.

Cider is so very food friendly. People like food, no—we freakin' love food, made by chefs, made with care from local ingredients. And cider is the very best partner, better than beer, yes, even better than wine. A proper farmhouse cider, with notes from the apple, the farm, and perhaps the barrel, has the complexity of fine wine. With a balance toward acid and a softness of flavor that stays out of the way of the dish. Bring a bottle of proper farmhouse cider to your next dinner party or BYOB, you will look like the old-world-new-smart-food-pairing-hero. I promise.

Cider has flavors. American cider, unlike wine and beer, is unbound by old-world tradition and purity laws. While many cider makers focus on English- and French-style farmhouse ciders, even more add fruit, hops, botanicals, honey, etc. Nothing refreshes like a pineapple cider on a Texas summer day. You like hops? We can do that. Rosé? We can do that too. A cider cocktail with blood orange and Italian bitters? It's in the can. So whatever your tastes, your mood, your occasion, we have a cider for you.

Cider comes from trees. Trees, dear friend, are my heroes. Trees shade and cool the earth. Their roots hold soil tight, preventing erosion. Trees are home to birds, bees, and small, cute, furry animals. Trees clean the air. They pull carbon out of the atmosphere and bury it in the ground, doing their bloody well best to save us from our worst habits. Tell all those scientists trying to figure out how to sequester carbon to just plant more trees. Yes, trees are our angels, and more trees means heaven on earth.

And our friends, those three friends from the beginning? Now it's tonight, not ten years ago. The first friend, an environmental attorney, orders a hoppy cider. The second, he's a chef, gets a rosé cider. And the third, she just gets a cider spritz. And everyone is happy.

Introduction

LET'S FACE IT: JUST TEN years ago, hard cider really wasn't quite a thing yet.

Expats watching rugby matches might have sipped a Strongbow instead of a Carling. And former foreign exchange students to France or Spain might have pined for it, seeing if obscure liquor stores might just carry it. Heck, plenty of people thought cider was only something preschoolers drank in sippy cups before naptime.

But if you picked up this book, you know that hard cider definitely is a thing—and it's very much a growing thing—and more and more people are discovering it every day. Hard cider sales have skyrocketed in the last decade, surging to become a $1.3 billion business, with a 600 percent increase in the number of cideries since 2011 and a 36 percent increase in production during the same time period, according to the latest (2019) Cyder Market annual survey. Its sales have outpaced both wine's increase and craft beer's growth, and it's even gaining notice in the cocktail sector, with plenty of cider bars popping up from coast to coast.

In fact, there are more than nine hundred craft cideries in forty-nine different states and Washington, D.C., and hundreds more producers worldwide. In fact, producers in the United Kingdom, Ireland, France, Spain, Canada, Germany, New Zealand, South Africa, and other places are exporting their ciders for the very first time to the United States because people are not only intrigued by it, but they're drinking more of it.

According to Carla Snyder, agricultural entrepreneurship and marketing educator at Penn State University, hard cider is the fastest growing segment of the craft beverage market, and over the last ten years it has been "the world's fastest growing beverage category." In fact, within the craft beverage segment, hard cider comes

in second only to IPAs. Within the United States, there are at least
18 million cider drinkers, and that number continues to grow.

But despite the fact that more and more of us are drinking
it, there's still some confusion over this blossoming alcoholic
beverage.

Some consumer polls reveal such conundrums about hard
cider. For example, some drinkers think Mike's Hard Lemonade
and Redd's Apple Ale are cider (no). Is hard cider a type of beer
(uh, no), or is it a category of wine (not really)? Is cider-beer a thing
(nope)? Are all ciders sweet (and, no, again)? What is perry, and is
it a type of cider (sort of)?

This book answers these questions—and others you didn't
know you wanted to have answered.

In the first chapter, we'll define what cider is and what it isn't.
We'll explore the common misconceptions that arise while drinking this tasty beverage, and we'll look at why the apple matters, how
cider is made, and which main categories of cider you might want
to explore.

While cider remains a cipher for some people, for much of our
American history, it was more common than clean drinking water,
so in chapter 2, Biting the Apple, we'll take a bite, er, sip of hard
cider history. The cider-drinking habits of our Founding Fathers
(and Mothers), Johnny Appleseed, and then cider's fall into obscu-
rity are all explored in depth.

We'll also take a look at cider's rebirth, and then we'll take a
look at the things that might help you better appreciate cider, from
its flavors and aromas to even the types of glasses to better enjoy
cider. If you enjoy traveling, skip ahead to chapter 5 to see where to
explore cider in the world, whether it's cider regions, cider bars, or
CiderCon.

If you're hooked on drinking cider, you might want to try your
hand at making your own. We will show you what equipment you
need, what ingredients you should have on hand, and how to safely
make a batch of hard cider in your house.

Because cider is so perfect for mixing with spirits, we dedicate
a single chapter to nothing but cider cocktails. Both modern and
historic cider cocktail recipes are included, as well as some basic

cocktail-making techniques and recipes for syrups, tinctures, and shrubs that will enhance your cider cocktails.

Finally, we'll take a look at pairing cider with food, as cider is perhaps the best beverage ever to pair with almost everything. We include what foods naturally pair well with cider, pairing rules to follow, as well as some recipes and techniques for cooking with hard cider.

Gathering apples for cider in Spain.

By the time you finish reading this book, you'll likely be ready to pass the first level of the Cider Certification Professional exam, the cider world's version of a sommelier certification.

In short, you'll be more than ready to get your cider on!

CHAPTER 1
Getting Your Cider Geek On— or, Cider 101

"It's indeed bad to eat apples.
It's better to turn them all into cider."
—Benjamin Franklin

CAN YOU PICTURE IT? Defining cider starts in your head. If you go to a pub in London, a bar in Asturias, or a restaurant in Normandy, if you order cider—*sidra* in Spanish or *cidre* in French— what you'll get is a glass of hard cider. And, two hundred years ago, if you were in an American tavern, that's also what you would get if you ordered cider.

But in the United States today, cider, without the modifying word *hard* preceding it, means unfermented or nonalcoholic apple juice in all of its forms, straight from an apple farm, bottled, and preserved to sit on a store shelf or secured in a sippy cup. While some folks might argue that there's a difference between nonalcoholic juice and cider (one is filtered and one is not), the main thing is that there is no alcohol in this beverage whatsoever.

Hard cider, on the other hand, most definitely refers to an alcoholic beverage. But the exact nature of this beverage, and a clear picture of what it is and what it isn't, as well as how to

A cider apple before it gets milled and pressed into juice for making cider.

properly categorize it, confuses people. Where should we classify it—in our brains, let alone on the menus at bars or shelves at liquor stores?

We know, for example, what wine is—whether it's an expensive Château Lafite Rothschild or white zin or your grammy's homemade rhubarb wine. Whether it's sweet or aged or tannic, with bubbles or without, red, white, or pink, we know what wine is. Even if it comes in cans, our brains already classify it as wine, not beer, and we have an underlying understanding that it is an alcoholic beverage made from grapes, even if we don't know how the heck it's made.

We also know what beer is—whether it's a Bud or Miller or some Exploding/Nearly Profane Named/Crazy IPA from your local craft brewery or your brother's homemade pale ale. Whether it is fruity or yeasty or sour, dark or light, mass-produced or micro-produced, in a bottle, a can, or on draft, we know what beer is. We know what it smells like, and we most likely know it's made with hops, even if we don't have a clue what hops are or why they're important to beer.

And we also know what spirits are, whether they're in the form of a shot at a college bar or a 20-year-old aged whiskey that costs more than a car payment, or your uncle's moonshine. We know you drink them straight or mixed in cocktails, and we also know how easily it is for some of us to get schnockered drinking them.

But, when we talk about hard cider, the definition that comes to mind isn't so clear. A picture might not automatically come into our heads. We might think of apples, but even the name cider often makes us first picture the stuff in sippy cups.

Additionally, many of us can name family occasions where our parents or grandparents drank wine, beer, or cocktails, and most of us remember the first beer we tasted at a college frat party or the first time we sipped wine at a wedding or the first shot a friend gave us on our 21st birthday. Additionally, we also likely can remember commercials, advertisements, and pop culture moments that are associated with these beverages.

But hard cider, though it is an ancient and once well-established beverage in our country, was lost through much of the last century, so we don't have these normative, cultural cues or memories that tell us concretely what it is.

Why Cider Gets Confusing

Cider being the new kid on the block is exciting, but it's also why people start to get confused about it. It has similarities in taste, serving styles, and packaging to both wine and beer, so the question is: is it like beer, or is it like wine? Or is it something else altogether?

A lot of times it's on the beer section of menus, and in some bars and restaurants, it's on the draft lines. Cider's also served in cans, in six-packs, and in 12-ounce beer-like bottles. It's also fizzy or effervescent. So, is it like beer?

But, then again, it's also sometimes served in 750-milliliter bottles like wine, and in some places, it's poured and served like wine. It's also made from fruit like wine is, and like some wines— sparkling and champagne wines—it's got bubbles. So, should cider be classified like wine?

Why Cider's Not "Cider Beer"

While cider shares some characteristics of both beer and wine, it is distinct from both beverage categories. But let's first discuss why cider's not beer or "cider beer," as some folks refer to it.

At its most basic level, hard cider is a fermented beverage made from apple juice. The juice can come from freshly pressed apples or straight juice (or in some commercial cases, apple concentrate, but more on that later in this chapter). But the keys here are *apples* and *juice*.

Some beers, Redd's Apple Ale chief among them, are flavored with apples, but beer manufacturing never starts with juice, it always starts with water. Grains, usually barley, are soaked with hot water in a process called mashing. The result is wort, which is then brewed with hops and/or spices, and then finally it is fermented with yeast.

When you're talking about the process of cider making, the juice gets fermented straight out of the pressing. Cider is never brewed; it is always fermented. While there may be differences among ciders in the length of time and the exact methods of fermentation, cider is always, always fermented, and it is never, ever brewed.

This is a key difference, because beer is always brewed. That means that *cider beer*, despite the term's common usage, is not a real thing. Even if it comes on tap or out of a can or is on the beer list of a bar menu, cider beer isn't a thing at all.

Cider is fermented from the juice or fruit of apples, just as wine is fermented from the juice or fruit of grapes.

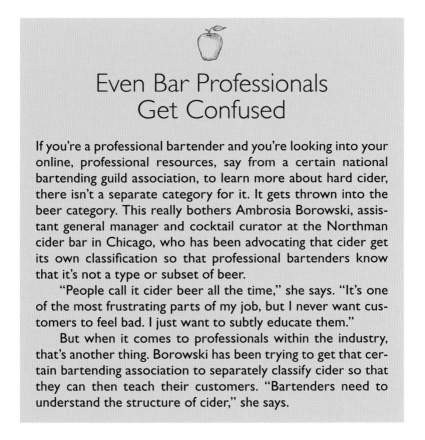

Even Bar Professionals Get Confused

If you're a professional bartender and you're looking into your online, professional resources, say from a certain national bartending guild association, to learn more about hard cider, there isn't a separate category for it. It gets thrown into the beer category. This really bothers Ambrosia Borowski, assistant general manager and cocktail curator at the Northman cider bar in Chicago, who has been advocating that cider get its own classification so that professional bartenders know that it's not a type or subset of beer.

"People call it cider beer all the time," she says. "It's one of the most frustrating parts of my job, but I never want customers to feel bad. I just want to subtly educate them."

But when it comes to professionals within the industry, that's another thing. Borowski has been trying to get that certain bartending association to separately classify cider so that they can then teach their customers. "Bartenders need to understand the structure of cider," she says.

Cider's Not Exactly Wine, Either

But cider isn't exactly wine. Like wine, it's made from the juice of fruit, and both are fermented alcoholic beverages, not brewed.

And the processes for making both cider and wine are more similar to each other than to the process for making beer.

There are, however, some key differences between hard cider and wine.

Hard cider's definitely not like the wine in that it's made from grapes—because grapes aren't used at all. But wine can be made from other fruits, including apples, so is hard cider interchangeable with apple wine?

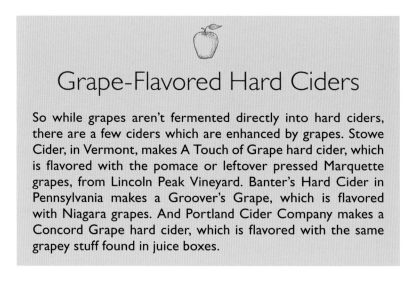

Grape-Flavored Hard Ciders

So while grapes aren't fermented directly into hard ciders, there are a few ciders which are enhanced by grapes. Stowe Cider, in Vermont, makes A Touch of Grape hard cider, which is flavored with the pomace or leftover pressed Marquette grapes, from Lincoln Peak Vineyard. Banter's Hard Cider in Pennsylvania makes a Groover's Grape, which is flavored with Niagara grapes. And Portland Cider Company makes a Concord Grape hard cider, which is flavored with the same grapey stuff found in juice boxes.

Though some will say there's really no difference between apple wine and hard cider, others will say there are two frequent distinctions between them: alcohol content and the bubble factor.

The first one is pretty easy to understand, and legally, it is how cider is defined. Cider contains less alcohol than wine does. It boasts a lower *ABV* or alcohol by volume. On the bottle or can of hard cider, it's often noted this way: X% ALC. VOL or X% ALC. By VOL.

Cider, on average, has an ABV of 3 to 7 percent. That's more akin to the ABV of beer than wine. The average ABV of wine runs higher, from 9 to 12 percent (or even higher), and that goes for both apple and vinifera wines.

In fact, according to the US government, hard cider is a fermented beverage with anything less than 7 percent alcohol by volume. Anything more than that, and the drink's called apple wine—and taxed at wine's higher rate. Now, some states, like Virginia, offer exceptions to this rule, and they individually allow ciders an ABV of up to 10 percent, but most states don't allow for this.

That's why plenty of cider makers make 6.9 percent alcohol by volume ciders—to stay within the federal tax guidelines. That also means that most ciders, like beer, are lower in alcohol than wine (and way lower than spirits).

Now, plenty of cider makers

German Hard Cider or Apfelwein?

Yes, German beer has conquered the world, and who doesn't enjoy a glass of Riesling from time to time, but though it's lesser known, it's no less delicious than these other two German beverages. Apfelwein, historically, actually dates back to Charlemagne, who was an enthusiast. It's mostly found in and around Frankfurt, and as its name suggests, is definitely treated similarly to wine. In fact, when the European Union decided that the term "wine" could only refer to grape-based beverages, which would have outlawed the use of the word "apfelwein," these good Germans were so upset that the etymological idea was nixed.

disagree with the government on this definition, and some cider makers make hard ciders that have more alcohol content in them than this arbitrary amount. In fact, some cider makers have been lobbying elected officials and pushing to have cider classified differently than both beer and wine, and they're looking to have the tax code changed to treat cider differently from wine or champagne. The proposed law is aptly named the Cider Investment and Development through Excise tax Reduction, or CIDER Act.

While most of us consumers don't care about tax classifications of various alcoholic beverages, we do generally want to know how much alcohol is in whatever we're drinking, and we want to know what to call it.

Bubble Regulation

The US government not only defines hard cider based on its alcohol content (7 percent or less), but it also defines exactly how much carbonation hard cider can have. If a hard cider has 3.92 grams of carbonation per liter, it's not classified as hard cider. It gets bumped up into the realm of champagne or sparkling wine.

Now, where this ABV stuff gets confusing is that there are some cider makers who make ciders that have an alcohol content of 7 percent ABV or higher—they just go ahead and pay the higher taxes, but still, they call those beverages cider, not wine, and it's really hard to say that there's a big difference between hard cider and apple wine.

But there's another thing to consider: the bubbles. Hard ciders are typically effervescent while apple wines may or may not be bubbly. This also can be confusing because some hard ciders are without carbonation, or are *still*.

Usually, though, hard ciders that don't have carbonation are labeled as such, and cider makers promote them as such.

In any case, the differences between apple wine and hard cider aren't clear-cut.

It's All about the Juice—or, Differences in Cider Ingredients That Help Define Cider

So, you have a picture of apples and fermentation and bubbles, so you know what cider is and what it tastes like, right?

Nope. If you've only tasted a cider made by a big maker or if you've only tasted cider from small craft cidery with its own orchard or if you've only tasted a modern cider flavored with some interesting herbs, well, they all taste so different from each other—sometimes to the point that they almost taste like completely, totally, absolutely different drinks. "Cider is an incredibly diverse industry, and the ways of making cider are extremely varied," says Michelle McGrath, executive director of the United States Association of Cider Makers. "We're a big tent, and the coolest thing about the cider industry is that we include people."

The differences are so great that some cider makers and enthusiasts think some ciders aren't really, well, ciders at all, and that they shouldn't even be labeled as such. Let's take a look at why the debate continues.

Cider apples come in different sizes, colors, and even shapes. Some are beautiful to look at, but a lot are on the ugly side.

The Types of Craft Cideries: First, Heritage Cider Makers—or, the Traditionalists

If you made hard cider the traditional way, it's all about the apples. You start with the apples, and you finish with the apples. And 9.9 times out of ten, the apples are apples you've grown or from orchards you've hand-selected.

Most heritage cider makers use apples that are cider apples—and many of these aren't what you'd find on a grocery shelf or at a farmers' market or even at those pick-your-own orchards. Many of them can be considered heirloom or antique or heritage apples, as they've been around for quite a while. But it's worth noting that some of these apples don't look visually appealing, and some of them taste even worse. Benjamin Franklin once wrote of their taste, "What you have told us is all very good. It is indeed bad to eat apples. It is better to make them all into cider."

On a Chemical Level: Cider Looks a Little More Like Wine

Scientists have analyzed the amount of polyphenol content of wine, beer, and hard cider. *Polyphenols* are the chemical compounds that add flavor, taste, aromas, and mouthfeel to these beverages, and many of them have health benefits. The average polyphenol content in beer ranges from 12 mg/100 ml (nonalcoholic beers) to 52 mg/100 ml (ales and stouts), with typical beers coming in around 28 mg/100 ml. For white wines, it's 30 mg/100 ml, and for red wines, it's about 210 mg/100 ml. A 2007 study, conducted at the University of Glasgow, analyzed the average phenolic content of several English hard ciders, and they ranged from 4.4 mg/100 ml to 155.9 mg/100 ml. So, hard ciders with more phenols tend to be closer, in chemical composition, to red wines than anything else. And while the study doesn't identify the hard ciders with the very low amount of phenolic compounds, one might guess that they're the unaged, more commercial variety, as phenolic compounds (in wine, anyway) increase in aging and when the wine is in contact with the skins longer.

"They're spitters," says Jessica Shabatura, founder and curator of howtomakehardcider.com, because you take a bite of these apples, and you'll spit them right out. But if you press them, then ferment their juice, well, ah, that's a different story.

Cider apples fall into four different categories: sharps, bittersharps, sweets, and bittersweets. These actual categories were established near Bristol, England, way back at the very end of the nineteenth century and the beginning of the twentieth century. There, the Long Ashton Research Station and the very beginnings of cider research were set up. It was here that researchers divided cidermaking apples up into these four types. These types were established based on the apples' differences in acids, tannins, and sweetness.

Acidity or acids are created from, well, acids, and in the case of apples, malic acid. Acid, as a flavor, is the tartness you taste when you bite into a lemon, for example. In the case of cider, acidity cuts through the sweetness or sugar levels, and it brings out the tannins.

Tannins are naturally occurring chemicals, usually found in the peels of fruit, and chemically speaking, they're considered polyphenols. But the taste of tannin is not chemical: it's a bitterness, a mouth-puckering dry feeling on your tongue. If you were to bite into a wet bag of black tea, that astringent sensation you'd get is from tannins. Tannins also occur in bar-

rels, which is why if you barrel-age a wine or a cider, you get additional tannins.

Sweetness, of course, comes from the natural sugar in apples, and while all apples contain sugar, some contain more than others, so let's start with the sweetest category, which is aptly called, "sweets." These apples are low in both acids and tannins, and they're the ones you're most familiar with. They're also known as *culinary* or *dessert* apples, or eating apples. Some apples within this category that are used in cider making include: Gala, Honeycrisp, Fuji, Empire, Golden Delicious, and Golden Russet.

Bittersweet apples are low in acid, but they're high in tannins. These apples add a great deal of complexity to ciders. Among the apples in this category are Dabinett, Yarlington Mill, Tremlett's Bitter, and Sommerset Red-streak.

Sharp apples boast a lot of natural acidity, and they're quite tangy on the palate. They're also pretty palatable, as they're also classified as culinary apples. Some of the apples in this category include: Granny Smith, Winesap, Jonagold, and Brown's Apple.

Bittersharps are intense, filled with high levels of both acidity and tannins. Some well-known bittersharps include: Kingston Black, Foxwelp, and Porter's Perfection.

Now, most traditional cider makers take apples from these four different categories, and they blend them to get the right taste, or rather, balance of sweetness, acidity, and tannin. It's worth noting that this is another difference between hard cider and wine: you're more likely to find single varietal wines—think chardonnay, cabernet sauvignon, Malbec—on the shelf than single varietal ciders.

But there are a few cider apples that, when in the hands of master cider makers, can make delicious, single varietal ciders. These apples include Kingston Black, Baldwin, Gravenstein, Winesap, and Newtown Pippin (it's also important to point out that both Gravenstein and Baldwin can be considered culinary apples, too).

Cider apples being transferred on conveyor belts before being milled and pressed.

These apples sometimes are called vintage apples, implying that they can by themselves make a singularly good cider.

Heritage cider makers, as their name implies, make cider the traditional way. They grow their apples and blend or not blend their apples using traditional methods and recipes, and they combine creative and critical thinking to get the most out of their fruit. Most, if not all, of the orchard-based cider makers in the United States could be considered heritage cider makers, and most of the European producers are heritage cider makers.

"Heritage cider producers are orchard based, thinking about the apple the way a winemaker thinks about the grape, to specifically express different characteristics of these apples," McGrath says, noting that often, their cider is usually more expensive than other ciders on the market.

That's not to say that they're not innovative, or that the methods of making their ciders are purely historical in nature. It's also not to say that they don't come up with unusual flavors or fruits to blend with their ciders. But what really makes them special is their access to and control over their fruit: they can pick and choose their blends of apples or use of single varietals.

They also know that no one else can make ciders exactly like them—because no one else grows apples like they do, in their particular region, with their particular soils and climates. And that gets us to terroir.

Pick a Peck of Apples

It takes a lot of apples to make just a little bit of cider. One bushel of apples, which weighs about 45 pounds, will only produce two, maybe three, gallons of cider. Now, consider this: one dwarf tree (the smallest size of apple trees) will produce only one and a half bushels of apples, which would make only three to four gallons of cider. A semidwarf tree grows about five bushels of apples or enough apples for 10–15 gallons of cider. And a regular apple tree yields 10 bushels of apples or enough apples to make 20–30 gallons.

Traditionalists and Terroir

The same apples, grown with similar agricultural management and then fermented and blended in the same proportions, will not taste the same if the apples are grown in a different area of the country, or, especially, the world. Terroir, or the impact climate (or even microclimates), land, and soil have on fruit make the fermented beverages taste different. The term is most often used to describe wine—for example, sauvignon blanc grapes grown in the Loire Valley of France yield an entirely different kind of wine than the sauvignon blanc grapes grown in New Zealand or sauvignon blanc grapes grown in California.

The same is true of Kingston Black apples grown in West County, England, or Kingston Black apples grown in Oregon or Kingston Black apples grown in Michigan.

Two things, however, differ when you're talking about terroir for grapes and terroir for apples. The first is, most hard ciders aren't made from single varietals like many wines; they're blends of different apples. The second is that most hard ciders aren't dated with vintages, and it's important to bring up vintages when talking about terroir because the same wines or ciders made from exactly the same fruit in exactly the same vineyards or orchards by exactly the same people don't taste exactly the same year to year.

Shabatura is currently working on a research project for an orchard in Arkansas, running treatments on different yeasts and temperatures to see how it affects the orchard's apples. "Apples from

the very same tree are different year to year, and I can measure the different tannin levels and sugar levels," she says. "It's going to be dependent on how cool the day was when the apples were picked, how rainy it was, and was there a dry, hot dip in the middle of the summer? All of that botany makes a difference in flavor. It's incredibly complex so with that in mind, we have to look at the things we can control."

Some cider makers are dating their blends and single varietals, and even those who aren't labeling their bottles or cans of cider with vintage dates, if they grow their own apples, they understand the terroir of their orchards. They also understand intrinsically why their own unique terroirs help them create unique ciders, and they speak of terroir just as winemakers describe it.

Mark Squires, a writer and wine reviewer for Robert Parker's *Wine Journal*, wrote about a discussion he had with Diane Flynt, owner of Foggy Ridge in Virginia. "What was more important was that what she was saying made automatic sense to a wine person," he described their conversation. "She sounded just like a wine geek. Only she was using apples and we don't consider apple wine to be real wine, do we? Yet . . . suddenly I was intrigued."

Another thing to look at when talking about terroir is what apples grow best under what conditions. Though you can find apples that can grow in many different conditions in many different climates, not every type of apple can grow in every type of climate or in every type of soil, and not every type of apple can grow well in different climates or soils.

Robert Purman, of Island Orchard Cider, grows his own apples on Washington Island in Lake Michigan before he makes them into cider and sometimes ages them into other cider-related beverages, like Pomona cider.

The Steps to Make Hard Cider

1. Harvest the apples. And leave the ones on the ground where they fall, as they likely harbor bacteria; sometimes the kind of bacteria that will make you sick, and sometimes just the bacteria that will make vinegar. In any case, forget the windfalls, and leave them for the squirrels.
2. Clean and sanitize the apples. There still might be dirt on the apples, and you don't want any leaves or twigs pressed with your cider.
3. Optional step: let the apples mellow or soften, called "sweating." Not every cider maker uses this process, and not every apple needs this extra ripening.
4. Mash the apples. Since you can't just squeeze juice out of an apple like you can an orange, you have to mill them down into a mush called pomace (this is also what the remains of pressing are called).
5. Press the pomace. Basically, the apple mush gets squeezed so the juice flows out.
6. Blend the juices. Since most hard ciders can be improved when the juices of several different kinds of apples are blended, this is where the artistry starts. Some cider makers blend the apples before pressing, others blend after pressing, and still others blend the different juices after they've been fermented. Cider makers often blend the juices based on sweetness, acidity, tannin or bitterness, and aroma, so that things taste and smell right.
7. Ferment the juice. Yeast is added to the pressed and blended juices, and it starts converting the sugars into alcohol. During this process, some cider makers will add extra sugar, yeast nutrients (things like thiamine that encourage yeast growth), and even extra tannins or acids to balance out their ciders' flavors. The process can take a few weeks to several months.
8. Age the cider. Some ciders are ready in a couple of weeks, but others spend months in a barrel or bottle to age the way wine is aged.
9. Package the cider or just drink it.

Robert Purman, who owns Island Orchard Cider with his wife Yannique, fell in love with the hard ciders of Normandy and Brittany, France. But when they decided to make hard cider and to grow their own apples in Wisconsin—on Washington Island in particular, which is a tiny island in Lake Michigan—they couldn't just select French apple varietals. "It was a long, slow process to determine which cultivars grow best," Purman says.

While Purman makes hard cider using French techniques and even uses French barrels to age some of his ciders, he grows a different mix of apples because the terroir of Washington Island is different from that of Normandy. "We always honor the apple first in everything we do," he says.

But not all cider makers grow their own apples, and that gets us into the second category of modern craft cider makers.

Things get a bit more complicated when you talk to modern cider makers. Some cider makers are adamant that their beverages are "cyder." The folks at Minchew's Real Cyder & Perry, for example, emphasize what they consider to be the differences between "cyder" and "cider." On their website, they declare: *Cyder* is rarely made, at least on a commercial scale. *Cider*, on the other hand,

Cider or Cyder?

Another point of confusion—or clarification, depending on which cider maker you talk to—is that sometimes "cider" is spelled "cyder." Now, technically, both words refer to an alcoholic beverage made from fermenting apples. But there are some interesting things about these words, both from history and implication. "Cyder," for example, can be considered an older version of "cider." But even if you go back historically, sometimes the terms were used interchangeably. One historical document—President John Adams's diary—shows that he sometimes used the term "cyder," and he sometimes used the term "cider," and he was talking about the same thing.

is. *Cyder* is made from a single pressing of a vintage fruit, rather like "extra-virgin" olive oil. *Cider*, the drink given to agricultural (laborers) well into living memory, was made from the cyder pulp being re-pressed at the rate of 10 gallons of water to 1 quart of pulp. This "long drink" was conspicuously different, not only in its alcoholic value, but also its taste. This type of cider could never mature in cask or bottle and was meant for general consumption, at a time when water was not always safe to drink.

Another cider maker, Blue Bee Cider in Virginia, makes one "cyder," and they call it "cyder," not "cider" because it is made using a recipe from the eighteenth century.

Windfall Cyder in Minnesota uses the antique spelling because founder and maker Rob Fisk says cyder is the more traditional spelling, and by using that term, he's indicating that his cyders are made in a more traditional, albeit elevated, style.

So, today, if it's cyder, not cider, it's probably more of a traditional style of drink.

Modern or Progressive Cider Makers: The Second Category

Since a lot of cider makers don't have their own orchards, they have to buy apples or juice from farmers. So, what kind of apples do they use?

Cider: The Legal Definition of Ingredients

You'd think that something called cider had to be mostly made, directly made, from the juice of apples. But legally, in the United States, up to 50 percent of the ingredients don't have to be. And in the United Kingdom, up to 65 percent of the ingredients can be something else.

Culinary apples. These are the SweeTango, Ambrosia, Red Delicious—basically any and all apples you'd be familiar with in your grocer's produce section or at a pick-your-own apple orchard. Now, if you visit an orchard or talk to a farmer, you'll know that within this category, some of these apples are better for baking, some are best used in applesauce, and some are just plain, good eating apples right out of the bag or the bushel.

If you're making cider, you might not want to use just apples that fall into the sweets and sharps category. Ideally, you'd want a blend like the heritage cider makers use, but since orchardists and farmers grow what they can sell and make a living from selling, you're at their mercy.

Cider apples, when you don't grow your own, can be prohibitively expensive, says Walker Fanning, owner and founder of Hidden Cave Cidery in Madison, Wisconsin. The reason cider apples can be so costly is that after Prohibition, there weren't too many orchards of these apples left, and most apple orchard farmers grow culinary apples because there's a much larger market for them. Fanning says he and other modern cider makers do their best to source the apples locally, at the best price they can get them, and then make the cider from this juice, without adding water back.

These ciders do, in a sense, taste of terroir in that they're made from the juice of local apples, but culinary apples tend not to have the variances in tannins and acids that cider apples do. "Modern cider makers are usually buying juice freshly pressed or buying apples and pressing them themselves," McGrath says. "Making their cider is less about the apples' character and more about other flavors and getting very innovative and creative about those."

So, how do they make balanced, delicious ciders? They experiment more with yeasts on the fermentation end, finding which

yeasts work with the juices to create a desired outcome. "All yeasts have a different preference of where they want to be" in fermentation, Fanning says. "Different yeasts impart different flavors (to the finished ciders)."

They also experiment on the blending side, too, using different sugars or honeys or maple syrup even, for sweetening, and they also incorporate different spices, hops, and other fruits to create different ciders as well.

It's worth noting that traditional cider makers also experiment with yeasts, sugars, and blending ingredients, but they start with the apples themselves whereas cider makers without orchards don't have that prerogative.

While most European cider makers have access to cider apples, some cider producers are specifically choosing to go the American, innovative route and only press culinary apples into their ciders. Hawkes Ciderie and Taproom in London is making its Urban Cider this way. Mattie Beason, owner of Black Twig Cider House in Durham, North Carolina, says it's ironic because so many modern cider makers in the United States would be using cider apples if they could.

"They would 100 percent be using bittersweets and bitter-sharps if they had access to them," he says. "It's interesting. We can't constrain ourselves because we don't have the fruit Europe has. At the same time, Europeans look at us and go 'Wow. How cool is that that they can make these fruit ciders and flavored ciders and really bring new flavors to the table.'"

Now, sometimes, these orchard-less cider makers also use apple juice concentrates, and this gets us to the next category of cider makers: commercial or larger-scale cider production.

Big Cider—or, the Third Category of Cider Makers

The line between modern or progressive cider makers and big cider makers is definitely blurred. But there is one point of argument that often, smaller-scale cider makers use in differentiating themselves from the big guys: it's what they use, or don't use, in cider making.

Some craft cider makers and connoisseurs say that mass-produced cider, made by very large companies, isn't really cider at all because the makers don't start with plain old apples. Instead of starting with apples, they start with apple juice concentrate, also known as apple concentrate.

"Heritage cider makers are using heritage or cider apples, and culinary fruit cider makers are using culinary apples, but even the

The Highlights of Making Apple Juice Concentrate

1. The first few steps of apple concentrate making are the same as regular cider making: the apples are harvested, sanitized, and then mashed or milled down into the pulp called pomace.
2. But instead of just pressing the pomace into juice, this apple mush is heated to at least 190 degrees Fahrenheit.
3. Then, enzymes are added for at least 30 minutes to break it down even more.
4. After the enzyme processes are finished, it goes through a heat extraction to remove the juice.
5. Then, the juice is filtered and heated again through a process similar to distillation, in which even more water is removed.
6. The resulting apple juice concentrate is very light in color, has virtually no smell, and offers very little apple flavor.
7. But through this process, another product is created: *apple essence*, which can be added back to the concentrate to add aromas and flavors.

culinary fruit people, because they are choosing to use fruit, are still showing an interest in the apple and an interest in a quality product," Beason says. "Then you have the third group, the ones making more mass-produced cider, and it's made from concentrate. They're getting concentrated apple syrup, and if they care at all, they're getting it from Europe rather than China, but those are the two major areas you get it from."

Apple juice concentrate sounds like it's just juice that's been boiled down so that it's more concentrated, or even stronger tasting. But that's not the case, and that's not the process.

So, because they're not using straight juice, they add water back, and they also often add additional sugar, too. Then, before it's fermented and bottled, flavorings, colorings, essences, and acids are added back in to produce something that tastes better. Since they're made of natural extracts, they're not always even labeled on the bottles or cans.

"They're alcopops," says Ambrosia Borowski, assistant manager of the Northman cider bar in Chicago.

Jessica Shabatura, an expert home cider maker, says that she personally wonders if, in the supply chain for cider making, it makes sense to transport juice laden with water or just concentrated juice. "Perhaps we need to concentrate on how we're doing the concentration versus whether concentration is good or bad," she says.

Some cider makers who use apple juice concentrate also add fresh or frozen whole juices to their products, and they only use the concentrate because of demand or expense. But it's important to note that while technically, they are natural, as all of their ingredients are derived from nature, they are processed. Jeff Alworth, a beer and cider writer and author, calls these products "constructed ciders."

"Rather, the takeaway for me is realizing how processed (apple juice concentrate) really is, and how manipulated ciders using it must by necessity be," Alworth writes in an article for *All About Beer* magazine. "It results in a consistent, mass market product that can be made year-round. If you're looking for the flavor of an orchard in your cider, though, you won't find it in products that use apple juice concentrate."

Cider's Relatives

While many people associate hard cider with beer or wine, cider has some closer relatives on the tree of alcoholic beverages. In fact, you could say they're on the same branch or nearby branches of that tree.

Cider's closest relative is *perry*. Perry is basically hard cider, but it's made from the juice of pears, not apples. Sometimes, it's called pear cider, but the better term to use is perry because there are pear ciders just like there are mango ciders and raspberry ciders. Pear ciders are apple ciders that are flavored with pear juice: they aren't based on fermented pear juices. But just like hard cider can be made from a variety of apples, perry can be made from a variety of pears.

Sugar, Glorious, Sugar

There's another step that also differentiates many mass-produced ciders. To get cider fermented to the exact right levels, they borrow a technique from winemaking called *chapitalization*. They pour in additional sugars or glucose into the juice mixture before it is fermented. If the post-fermented cider is too high in alcohol, they could then just cut it with water to get the exact ABV they desired.

Beason says that there are people out there who are using concentrate who make good cider. "But there certainly is a debate out there," he says. "Go to someone using heritage apples from their own orchard, and they're creating a very intended product. They don't think too highly of the people buying essentially a concentrated apple syrup and reconstituting it with water to produce their cider. Those two products are two very, very different things."

There's room, however, in the cider market for these vastly different ciders, just as there's room in the beer market for conglomerate light beers and microbrewed craft ales. "Think of these ciders as gateways," Beason says. "These producers are making a product that is accessible and inexpensive, and they are bringing people to the table. If you talk to some of them, they will tell you just this—that they don't hang on to their customer base . . . who move on to a more intended product."

Beason thinks that these producers have a necessary place in the cider world. "Absolutely, you need those Miller Lites to get to Bell's Two Hearted," he says. "You're not going to get very many people starting with Bell's Two Hearted. For Foggy Ridge or Farnum Hill (ciders), most people need something to get them started. Because these ciders are intentional, they're a little more challenging.

"They challenge the palate, they challenge the mind, and it's no different than me growing up thinking broccoli was the worst thing ever . . . until I was twenty-five, and somehow my palate changed, and with my palate changing, all of a sudden, broccoli became something I think was fantastic. We all graduate."

Perry-making pears, like the bittersharps, sharps, and bitter-sweets in the apple varieties, often do not taste as sweet or sumptuous as culinary pears. Perry pears are often harder to grow and fussy, so since more pears are grown for eating rather than perry-making, culinary pears are also used to make perry. Many hard cider makers also make perry, and these makers fall into all three classifications of hard cider makers.

Another beverage related to hard cider is apple brandy. Some apple brandies, made in Normandy, are also known as calvados. Calvados is made when you distill hard cider into an eau-de-vie, or a clear, colorless fruit brandy, which is then aged in casks. It is sort of like an apple version of cognac—and it's delicious by itself or when mixed in cocktails.

American apple brandies, by contrast, aren't rigidly controlled by rules and location. Some of them are aged, and some of them are unaged. Whether they're aged or unaged, they're great sippers by themselves, but they also lend themselves quite deliciously to cocktails.

Then there's pommeau, which is when apple brandy gets blended with unfermented apple juice, and then the mix is aged in oak barrels, creating a luscious, sweet apple liqueur, which tastes great all by itself. It also, like calvados, can be blended into cocktails, but it's more often used as a digestif, or a drink to help you digest after a meal. Though this is traditionally made in Normandy, American hard cider makers like Island Orchard Ciderie, South Hill Cider, and Carr's Ciderhouse are now making their versions of this classical liqueur; it's also worth noting that these smaller, American cider makers often sell out of their pommeau pretty quickly.

Another close relative of hard cider is ice cider or *cidre de glace*, which was created first by cider makers in Quebec about twenty-five years ago. This is cider's version of ice or dessert

Eden Specialty Cider's ice ciders are aged outside in Vermont's cold winters.

wine, and it's made by letting the apples freeze on the tree before they're pressed. Ice cider tastes like liquid apples when it's made right, and oh, is it good! There are only a couple of American cider producers who make it the traditional way—by using the natural, hard cold of the outside instead of making them inside of freezers, and one of the best is Eden Specialty Ciders, which is located in northern Vermont, just a stone's throw away from the Canadian border.

"The primary difference between ice ciders made by using outdoor temperatures is the outside has this natural temperature variation," says Eleanor Leger, who founded Eden with her husband, Albert. "The average temperature from December to January (here in Vermont) is 18 degrees, but it can vary from minus 35 to plus 35, which is a variation of 60 degrees. That really helps the flavors, acids, and sugar concentration develop, and it yields a much more intense (overall) flavor than if you just throw the cider in a freezer."

Applejack sounds like it would be a close relative of hard cider, and initially, that's how it started out. Applejack originally was an American version of apple brandy, and colonial cider makers would

make it by setting their barrels of hard cider out in the
cold. The cider would freeze.
What wasn't frozen was thus, a
"jacked up" version. But what
it was—and what defines it—
changed in the late 1960s.

Around that time, color-
less spirits like vodka and gin
were growing in popularity, so
whiskey makers started mak-
ing some blended, lighter spirits, and then the federal government
got involved in defining what it was. To be called applejack, a spirit
has to have at least 20 percent distillate of apple brandy that's then
blended with a neutral spirit, and that blend has to be aged for at
least four years in used bourbon barrels.

Applejacks tend to have less apple flavor than pure apple brandies, but they're still quite delicious, and they're also amazing in
cocktails. Applejack takes a star role in the classic cocktail, the

Laird's AppleJack

The oldest family-run distillery in the United States is Laird's—
and they've been distilling straight apple brandy and blended
apple brandy with spirit for centuries. Their official "commercial transactions" date back to 1780, but they've been distilling
brandy since 1698. It's worth noting that George Washington
was a fan of their spirits, and he asked the Laird family for their
recipe for applejack, which he took with him home to Mount
Vernon in 1760, before the United States was even a country.

The ninth and tenth generations of the Laird family continue to distill these delightful spirits in Monmouth County,
New Jersey, and they make both a straight applejack brandy
and an applejack brandy that's blended with whiskey. Both are
smooth and delicious on their own—especially the 100 percent apple brandy—but they are equally impressive in cocktails.

Jack Rose (see chapter on cocktails), which combines it with grenadine and either lime or lemon juice. But when it was popular in the 1920s and 1930s, it was made with applejack when it was apple brandy—not a blend of apple brandy and a neutral spirit like it is today.

While applejacks have a long history, a newer cider category of spirits is apertifs. Apertifs are a category of bitter liquors that are often made with wine—vermouths and amaros, for example—but Eden Specialty Ciders are now making American-made, cider-based apertifs called Orleans. Orleans comes in three different varieties: Bitter, which is infused with dandelion, gentian root, red current, and angelica (it's in the same genre as Aperol or Campari), Wood, which is infused with spruce tips, wild mint, wormwood, sweet gale, and raw honey (as a riff on Chartreuse and Absinthe), and Herbal, which contains basil and hyssop.

The Orleans aperitifs are made from all real ingredients—no artificial flavorings or colorings—and they also contain no added high-fructose corn syrup or processed sugars, so they're not very sweet. They also, like Eden ciders, are made with all locally sourced ingredients. "They're not direct analogues to other products that are out there, and while they're easiest to use as a replacement for Aperol or Campari in a cocktail recipe, they're not exact replacements, it sometimes takes a little tweaking in a recipe" says Eleanor Leger, who founded the Vermont ciderie and orchard with her husband Albert.

Eleanor and Albert Leger, owners of Eden Specialty Cider.

CHAPTER 2
Biting the Apple

"The tarter the apple, the tastier the cider."
—Beverly Lewis

THE HISTORY OF HARD CIDER starts with the apple, or rather, when we humans started consuming and then cultivating apple trees. The modern domestic apple is classified as *Malus pumila*, and while there are many varieties under this umbrella classification, they all are part of the rose family, as are pears, strawberries, plums, and raspberries.

The reason why this classification is important is that scientists, rather recently, have confirmed that our modern apples descend from a wild type of apples found in Kazakhstan called *Malus sieversii*. Previously, there had been some debate, as well as conflicting studies, as to whether the predecessor of modern apples came from this Kazakhstan apple or a European crab apple (with classification *Malus sylvestris*). Scientists, using DNA sequencing, have definitively determined that the apples we grow today for eating and hard cider making all descend from these apples, grown in the forests of the Tien Shan mountain range. These mountains sit outside the city of Almaty and border China.

What's in the Name of Almaty

Before the city came to be known as Almaty, it was called "Alma-Ata," which means "father of apples." It's an apple of a name for the ground zero of apple growing.

What's unusual about the forest in these mountains is that they're absolutely filled with apple trees—so much that the floors of the forests seasonally are covered by a carpet of fallen fruits. And there are dozens of different kinds of wild and ancient hybrid apples. It's so lush and beautiful and aromatic that some folks call it the Garden of Eden.

Though apples are mentioned by name in other legends—in Greek mythology, the Hesperides sisters guarded Hera's golden apples with the dragon Ladon, who eventually was slain by Hercules; the Norse goddess Iduna grew special apples in an

A Michigan cider orchard.

orchard, and the other gods achieved immortality by eating them, and there's even a story in Celtic folklore about a man who was able to eat for a year in just one apple—apples are not, in fact, mentioned in Genesis at all.

When Eve Picked an Apple—or Did She?

If you actually read the Book of Genesis (in the Torah and in the Old Testament of the Bible), you might notice in the story of the Garden of Eden, in the whole drama of Eve, Adam, that nasty snake, and the forbidden fruit Eve picked from the tree that was in the middle of the garden, the exact type of fruit she picked was never actually specified.

The idea of apples as *the* forbidden fruit started out in the fourth century A.D. when the pope at the time, Pope Damasus, had his leading theologian, Jerome, translate the Hebrew Bible into Latin. In the Hebrew Bible, the word used is *peri*, which is a generic term for any kind of fruit. It could be figs, apricots, grapes, pomegranates, plums, peaches . . . peri could mean just about anything. But Jerome decided to translate *peri* as *malus*, which in Latin not only means apple, but more importantly, *malus* means "evil." Now, what complicates this translation a little bit more is that *malus* doesn't just refer to actual apples—it also refers to any fleshy, seed-bearing fruit.

So while this is the first reference to the fruit as possibly an apple, this reference could also mean a pear or a fig, and if you ever get to the Vatican City and visit the Sistine Chapel, you'll notice that Michelangelo painted Adam and Eve beside a fig tree.

Then, in the early sixteenth century, German artist Albrecht Dürer depicted them next to an apple tree, which other artists then replicated in their work. And a certain writer named John Milton, in his famous *Paradise Lost*, retells the story of the fall, and he refers to the fruit, in his opening lines, as just "the Fruit," but he later twice calls it an apple.

Milton, who was not just a poet but a scholar of Latin, likely recognized Jerome's terminology and double-intentioned meaning, so he chose to repeat it, but in English, not Latin. Now, what complicates things, again, is that in Milton's time, the term apple referred not just to apples, but like the word *malus*, indicated any fleshy, seed-bearing fruit. But eventually, as the English language evolved and as subsequent generations read Milton's classic poem, an apple meant just an apple, and so, an apple's been the forbidden fruit of choice ever since.

Because Almaty was an important city along the Silk Road, an ancient trading route, traders and travelers would enjoy the fruit, and they took back with them the seeds, which of course, spread around the world. Perhaps the earliest evidence of eating apples are some carbonized apple remains found in prehistoric lake dwellings in Switzerland.

Now, here's also why the apples spread elsewhere developed differently. Eventually, people came to understand that if you enjoyed the apples of one tree, planting seeds from apples of those tree didn't create fruit replicas of that original tree. Instead, the new tree's fruit often were quite different from those of the parent trees. Scientifically speaking, apples are considered *heterozygous*, which means that the genes in the seeds of an apple express themselves differently than those of their parents.

Ancient farmers who wanted to cultivate certain types of apples developed a technique called *grafting,* in which they'd take a cutting from a tree they'd like, and then they'd cut a notch into another tree and plop it in. The ancient Romans, Babylonians, Chinese, and Egyptians all grafted.

But grafting isn't the only technique that had to be developed to make hard cider. Other technological advances also had to be made. While modern historians believe we've been drinking fermented beverages for at least nine thousand years or so, hard cider was definitely not the first fermented booze to be sipped.

Why? Squeeze a grape, the juice pours out. Squeeze a citrus, again, the juice pours out.

But mash an apple . . . you get apple mush. To get the juice, you needed to grind and press the apples, and it wasn't until grinders and pressers were developed that hard cider came about.

The Romans Invented Cider . . . or Did They?

Now, following the apple's spread throughout Europe, Asia, and even Africa, by 1500 B.C., apples were being cultivated and planted, as an ancient Mesopotamian tablet details the sales of an apple orchard. There also are writings and evidence that apples were grown in ancient Egypt and Greece. But, when exactly did apple growing evolve into the making of booze?

There are basically three competing stories of who invented hard cider. One story supposes that the Romans invented cider, as they already were using presses to make olive oil, and just repurposed them for cider. They were technologically advanced for the time— and they also had immense bureaucracies and armies in place for not just conquering peoples, but also for spreading such technological advancements throughout the Roman Empire.

Spanish ciders are aged in giant barrels, just the way they've been made for centuries.

We know for sure that by the first century A.D., Pliny the Elder had written about the Romans making apple wine and perry.

Another theory presupposes that the Romans weren't the original cider makers. This theory posits that the Romans didn't start making wine from apples until after they got to the British Isles, where they first tasted cider, and then decided to make it their own (just to keep the dates straight, the Romans invaded Britain in 55 B.C.).

But the third legend has it that it wasn't the Brits who inspired the Romans to adopt cider making: it was the Spaniards in Asturias who taught them about hard cider. Asturias, which remains a fervent cider-making and cider-drinking region to this day, is located on the northwest coast of Spain. Though the Romans had conquered much of the Spanish peninsula, it wasn't until 25 B.C., that they finally took over this final region.

Now, this final conquering is after the Romans invaded Britain, but there's an earlier, written reference to cider making in Asturias. The Greek philosopher Strabo wrote in 60 B.C. that cider was made in this region. But there is one challenge with this reference: Strabo uses the word "zytho," which he also uses, in the same writing, to refer more clearly to beer. Others argue that zytho simply refers to any alcoholic beverage that isn't wine made from grapes, and that clearly because apples, not barley, were being cultivated, it has to be cider that he was mentioning. This argument is bolstered by that Roman foodie Pliny, who also visited and wrote about Asturias in the first century A.D. He described apple wine as the drink of the area.

Now, whether it was the Romans, the Asturians, or the Brits who invented cider (and maybe all three invented it around the same time), cider making itself goes back at least two thousand years.

Wars, Trade, and Climate Change Influenced Cider Making

After the Roman Empire fell by the fifth century A.D., cider making could have completely fallen by the wayside, but the monks kept apple growing and cider making alive in much of Europe through the Dark Ages. It also should be noted that in some areas, notably Asturias, cider making never stopped completely, and there are records throughout the Middle Ages documenting orchards and cider production.

Where Does the Term "Cider" Come From?

What's up with the term "cider" to refer to a wine-like beverage made from apples? The best guess is that the Latin word "*sicera*" could have evolved into cider in English, *sidra* in Spanish, and *cidre* in French. *Sicera* evolved from the Greek term "*sikera*," which referred to any boozy beverage that wasn't wine, and it could have evolved from the Hebrew word "*shekar*," which meant the same thing.

A few things happened, though, to rectify cider's historical course. The first is Emperor Charlemagne, by the late eighth century, actively encouraged cider makers to, well, make cider. In fact, he issued an edict to that effect.

Cider making, however, paled compared to production of beer and wine. At one time, grapes were grown as far north as England to make wine. Then, a climate crisis occurred: in the thirteenth century, a mini ice age happened, and the temperatures permanently changed for the colder. That's when cider making really got underway, and the most famous regions of cider (excluding Spain—where it never fell out of favor) were firmly established in England, France, and Germany.

Over the centuries, cider making improved, spread, and flourished, in part, due to wars, conquests, and trade. For example, in England, it was the Norman conquest that introduced new and different cider-making apples to the isle, renewing interest in the drink. Also, whenever England went to war with France, French wine fell out of favor, and thus, cider's popularity (and obviously, availability) grew.

And in Normandy, cider making was refined in the fifteenth century due to a Spanish gent named Guillaume D'Ursus. D'Ursus hailed from the Basque cider-making region, and he ended up in Normandy, where he had been granted some estates by the king. D'Ursus grafted new-to-the-region apple varieties, and he improved apple cultivation techniques. Because the Bay of Biscay was a big trade route between France and Spain, cider making and apple cultivation grew.

The practice of grafting to preserve good cider apples led to the establishment of cider apple varieties, and by the sixteenth century, there were more than sixty named cider-making varieties in Normandy alone. Improvements in making and especially in the pressing of the pomace also occurred, and that in turn encouraged more cider production.

Cider Making Flourishes in England . . . and then Gets Exported to America

As mentioned, the Norman Conquest of 1066 brought new apple varieties, and thus better cider making, to England. From this time on, apple cultivating grew. Just a century later, cider became almost as popular as ale, and it also, described in deeds and sales transactions, became a way to pay rent and church tithes. It even became a way to pay farmworkers—so much that if a land owner made great cider, that was attractive in hiring and retaining workers. Cider as part of a paycheck was a way of life on some farms until the practice was outlawed in 1878!

Cider and apples are mentioned in plenty of old manuscripts. In *Encyclopedia*, published in 1470, Bartholomeus Anglicus dedicated an entire chapter to apples. "Malus the Appyll tree is a tree yt bereth apples and is a grete tree in itself . . . and is gracious in sight and in taste and virtuous in medecyne. Some beryth sourysh fruyte and harde, and some right soure and some right swete, with a good savoure and mery."

Though ale-making grew in popularity and improved in the 1500s, when hops were introduced (they improved the taste and preservation of brews), cider making never truly fell out of favor.

The climate in Southwestern England was, and remains, especially good for apple growing, so apple growing—and cider making—spread. Noted English gardener and writer John Evelyn described this landscape as one gigantic orchard, as the apple trees from one farm just seemingly flowed into the next.

As it grew in production, gardeners and orchardists refined their techniques, and they also cultivated and developed certain apples for cider production. By the seventeenth century, orchards and cider making were flourishing, and most farmhouses were built with cellars to keep cider cool. Orchards were planted with widely spaced trees so that farmers could grow crops in between them or allow their sheep to graze, and since the apples weren't often ready for harvest until October, after other crops came in, cider making was a natural transition after harvest.

And they used practically every bit of the apples. Once pressed, the pomace would be soaked with water and then re-pressed into a lightly boozy drink called *ciderkin* or *water-cider*. Ciderkin was preferable to consume over water because water was often contaminated and made people sick. Afterward, the leftover pomace became food for farm animals. Old or dying apple trees were also cut down and used for fuel.

During fuel shortages—and in the late 1500s and early 1600s there was a shortage of wood for use as fuel, as well as restrictions on importing wood—cider making flourished because its fermentation didn't require heat, which is how beer is brewed.

Cider consumption was so high, scholar and writer John Beale wrote that by the mid-1600s, "Very few of our cottagers, yea, very few of our wealthiest yeomen, drink anything else (but cider) in the family save on very special festivals."

Cider-making presses were evolving as well, with horses grinding apples into cider, and with the advent of the industrial revolution, steam and hydraulic presses for cider were also developed to press apples.

Although most cider was made and stored in wooden barrels, putting cider into bottles became a thing after Lord John Scudamore started bottling them, using the champagne method, around 1640. Scudamore, a courtier of the king and former ambassador to France, also was one of those English gents dedicated to the development and classification of new and better cider apples, and he classified some 350 types. He is also credited with identifying the famed Herfordshire Redstreak apple, which was celebrated as an exquisite cider-making apple.

Throughout this time, English gentlemen who also made cider kept and published scrupulous (yet sometimes conflicting) records of cultivation, varieties, and making techniques. Even smaller farmers kept records.

And these records also show when these cider-drinking Englishmen took it to America, too.

Cider Making Takes Root—and then Flourishes—in the New World

The first English settlers in America brought with them their cider-drinking habits. Perhaps the most celebrated account of cider is that of the *Mayflower*. During its famous sixty-six-day voyage across the Atlantic Ocean in 1620, its crew and passengers suffered many setbacks and hardships, including encountering a very bad storm about halfway through the crossing. This storm caused one of the main support beams of the ship to crack, and it was repaired with the help of a giant metal screw, which helped raise the beam back into place. There are various accounts as to what this big screw was, and some accounts say that it was part of a cider press (others say it was a jackscrew used to help build houses). What we do know for sure is that on their journey one of the Pilgrims' most sanitary choices for drink was hard cider; the other two were aqua vitae (hard spirits) and ale.

We also know that just a few years later (likely in 1623), the Reverend William Blaxton (sometimes spelled Blackstone) planted the very first apple orchard in Boston, in the area now known as Beacon Hill. Blaxton, who was a minister for the Church of England, either didn't get along with the Puritans who later moved there or ran into some disagreements with colonial authorities in the area, so he decided to move (reportedly after some of the Puritans burned down his house) in 1635. Instead of staying in what would become Massachusetts, he moved 35 miles south and became the first settler of what would become Rhode Island. Again, he established orchards, and he also cultivated the very first American apple variety, the Yellow Sweeting, or Blaxton's Yellow Sweeting, which would later become known as the Rhode Island Greening, or Sweet Rhode Island Greening (even though it's more tart than sweet). It was discovered in his orchard in the mid-1600s.

Another early American apple was the Roxbury Russet (which some accounts say started out as the Yellow Sweeting), which was discovered as another chance seedling in a Roxbury orchard, sometime around when Blaxton left Boston (so it's possible but unverified that he planted it or it came from seeds from another of his plantings).

Though there were native crab apple trees in America, those were too sour for eating or drinking. English settlers did bring whole apple trees and grafts to put on trees, but a lot of these trees didn't survive the harsher winters of the New World, nor did these Old World trees survive the continued freezing temperatures and

A Famous Tree Grows in the East Village (and Another One Grows in Massachusetts)

Now, some grafted trees from Europe did survive, and one famous farmer was none other than Peter Stuyvesant, who became the first director general or governor of New Amsterdam. Stuyvesant had a farm or "bowery" in what was New Amsterdam, now New York City. In 1647, a young French pear tree, of the Summer Bon Chretien variety (possibly a parent to the Barlett pear), was shipped in a barrel from Holland and given to him at his home. This is the first recorded instance of a grafted tree coming to America, and it stood, blossoming and bearing fruit, for more than two centuries on the corner of 3rd Avenue and 13th Street in New York City until 1866, when a runaway delivery wagon crashed into it. Though this was definitely a pear tree, in some historical books and articles, it's described as an apple tree, and this confusion could have come from the fact that Stuyvesant was an avid collector of many different kinds of fruit trees in his garden, including apples. A plaque commemorates this pear tree, and in 2003, another pear tree was planted on the site. Though his original tree did end up getting cut down, graftings from this tree were planted throughout the Hudson Valley by Dutch settlers so in a sense, the tree does live on.

Now, while Stuyvesant's pear tree is arguably the most famous of historic American pear trees, it wasn't the oldest of record, which belonged to another colonial governor, that of John Endicott, governor of Massachusetts. Endicott grew an Endicott pear tree in 1632, but it's not known if it was grown from the seed of an imported tree or an actual imported tree. Unlike Stuyvesant's pear tree, the Endicott pear survived hurricane damage in 1804, 1815, 1934, and vandalism in 1964. The tree still lives on today, making it the oldest cultivated fruit tree in North America.

frosts in spring. But once these settlers planted seeds, these new trees took root, and both apple growing and cider making planted strong roots in their new home. As you know by now, the seeds from one tree produce new trees that are often quite different from its parent tree, so new American apple varieties began blossoming. Some settlers also took the leftover pomace from cider making, and they spread it on their fields, so that, too, encouraged new varieties to spring forward. "The land is the finest for cultivation that I ever in my life set foot upon, and it also abounds in trees of every description," wrote Henry Hudson in his journal in 1609.

A Cider a Day Keeps the Doctor Away

Hard cider wasn't just a healthier beverage to drink than water: proponents believed that it could treat gout, colic, bladder stones, laryngitis, fevers, and rheumatism. People also believed it could ease digestion, and they especially believed it led to longer living. In the *Massachusetts Agricultural Repository and Journal*, volume 1, published in 1799, a man by the name of Lazarus Redstreak wrote: "The beer of the best quality may be suitable for invalids and particularly for weak stomachs, too weak for solid food (reader here is no contradiction) than cyder. Cyder is, however, to be preferred to beer for laborers. Experience shows that the use of it consists with sound health and long life. Our habits are settled in favor of it. The New-Englanders are the longest livers. Why then try an innovation so difficult, so doubtful, to say the least, in point of health and economy, as the substitution of beer in the place of cyder? No then let us go and plant orchards as our forefathers did; and if we can, by God's blessing live as long and as well, and leave as good examples, and as precious institutions to our children as they did to us."

Just as in the Old World, less-than-sanitary-water made hard cider a drink not just of choice but of healthful necessity. Contaminated water caused all sorts of diseases including typhoid, dysentery, and cholera. Clean water, known as *tea-water* because it was suitable for making tea, was available, usually on the outskirts of cities, and laborers known as tea-water men would pump it out of wells or other clean water sources, keg it, and then transport it to the city. Tea-water, which was also used as plain old drinking water, was more expensive, however, than booze.

While beer and wine were often more popular than cider in Europe, cider was king in the colonies, as it definitively outranked both of them in popularity, becoming the most American of all beverages.

Cider became more popular, in part, because English ales were expensive to import, and when they made it across the Atlantic, they didn't always stay fresh or delicious. In the less than sterling storage conditions, the beer sometimes spoiled, becoming at best undrinkable and at worst lethal. The colonists did import hops and barley malt to make beer, but again, they were expensive, and there were often shortages of them.

So the colonists did try to make malt out of other ingredients, primarily maize (or corn). They also made brewing worts or beer starters out of molasses, persimmons, peaches, pumpkins, peas, maple sap, and even corn stalks. But ales made from malted corn stalks never caught on. "The richer sort brew their beer with malt, which they have from England . . . the poorer sort brew their beer with molasses and bran," wrote planter Robert Beverly.

Grape cultivation and wine making in the early colonies also weren't too fantastic. In Virginia, which is often noted to be the birthplace of American wines, some farmers were reasonably successful in planting grapes, but in the more northern colonies, there just wasn't the right climate for vinifera

Vinifera grapes

The species of grapes that get made into wine; *Vitis vinifera* is a separate species of grapes from table grapes; vinifera grapes have thicker skins and are juicier than table grapes, making them better suited for wine production.

grapes. Of the wines that did get fermented, many were quite bitter, and they didn't travel well. To support their wine-drinking habits, wine was, of course, then imported from France, Portugal, and other places in Europe, making it more expensive and less available.

But apples—ah, apples grown from seeds—these fruit trees flourished just about everywhere, and there were settlers in all original 13 colonies growing apples, from New England all the way down to Georgia. By 1775, one out of ten farms in New England boasted apple orchards and had cider-making operations on-site. The three largest cider-producing regions in the colonies were: Virginia, New England (and in particular, Massachusetts), and New Jersey. New Jersey produced the most cider commercially, and Newark, in particular, was a city known for its apples and some of the best cider in the country. The city's most celebrated apple was the Harrison, a small yellow apple with black spots. Cider made with Harrison apples tasted rich and fetched higher prices in New York. The Harrison itself was discovered in the early 1700s in an orchard owned by Samuel Harrison. It was first called the Osborne, then the Long Stem, and then finally the Harrison. In 1817, William Coxe wrote that, "This is the most celebrated of the cider apples of Newark in New Jersey." It was so good it was once called "the champagne of Newark."

Though some specific types of apples, including the Harrison, were prized—and thus grafted and cultivated, especially by gentlemen gardeners or collectors—most of the apples grown for both cider and eating were the result of seedlings. Seedlings, by their varied nature, were suitable for cider making since cider making

The Harrison's Rebirth

So if an apple made a cider so delicious, so celebrated and so famous, then what happened to it? While Harrison apples were flourishing in Newark and its surrounding towns in the early 1800s, by the late 1800s, they were rare. Joseph Folsom wrote in 1918 that these once common apples were crowded out by development, "Houses are built where they formerly grew." Urbanization not only cut down apple trees, but consumers moving to cities drank more beer than cider. Then Prohibition happened, and not only did cider consumption not make a comeback, cider apples like the Harrison became quite rare.

In 1976, Paul Gidez, a Vermont orchardist, who knew of the Harrison's fame, decided to search for it, and he found one at an old cider mill and took graftings from a tree that was later ripped out for a garden. Gidez now has 250 Harrison trees in his orchard.

Other orchardists and cider consultants from Virginia also became enthused about the apple, and they did their own searches and later graftings. Tom Buford, an orchardist who is considered a father of the Virginia cider movement, calls it the "most enigmatic apple" he's ever dealt with. And Diana Flynt, owner of Foggy Ridge Cider in Virginia, says its juice, which is so thick and viscous and packed with an intense apple flavor, carries over into any ciders made with it.

And today, the Harrison is being replanted in New Jersey, and New Jersey cider makers are using it when they can.

is a blend of different apples. The colonialists didn't care if their ciders changed a bit in taste from year to year, but the greater benefit to seedlings is that because some of them blossomed and bore fruit at different times, they extended the growing season.

But whether by graft or by seedling, by 1850, there were a whopping one thousand different varieties of apples recorded, and most of these apples were, of course, cider apples, not eating kinds.

Cider consumption in early America was, in a word, huge. It's hard to picture just how big of a thing cider drinking was. The most modern consumers might look at it as soft drink consumption was in the late 1990s or the Starbucks-driven gourmet coffee consumption that continues today. Except, some people never drank soft drinks, even in the days that McDonald's supersized things, and some people—especially children—never drink coffee. In the 1800s America, everyone, simply everyone, drank cider.

A single village outside of Boston preserved about 10,000 barrels of cider in just 1726. By 1767, people were consuming, on average, more than thirty-five gallons per person a year. People often started their days with a pint of hard cider for breakfast, and they continued to drink it throughout the day. And, of course, it wasn't just adults drinking hard cider. Children drank cider, and they also sipped the more watery ciderkin.

Sometimes, colonists imbibed too much hard cider, and by the 1660s, regulations about public drunkenness were enacted in Massachusetts, Maryland, and Virginia. In 1676, Nicholas Spencer, clerk for the Virginia House of Burgesses (the first democratically elected legislative body in the colonies), believed that the drinking of too much hard cider was a cause of tobacco riots at the time. "All plantations flowing with syder, soe unripe dranke by our licentious inhabitants, that they allow no tyme for its fermentation but in their braines."

Cider, as back in England, was also used as a form of payment. Currency itself was scarce, so, very often, colonists used hard cider to pay their bills. In fact, construction crews who built some of the earliest roads in America were paid in hard cider and applejack!

According to the book, *A History of Horticulture in America to 1860*, "From the founding of Jamestown to the time of George Washington and Thomas Jefferson, on down to that of Robert E. Lee, every plantation owner made cider, drank cider, and bragged about his cider."

But hard cider wasn't just imbibed straight or distilled into spirits: it was also transformed into apple cider vinegar, which became the most popular condiment in the colonies. Apple cider vinegar also was used to pickle vegetables and fruits, which preserved them and allowed colonists to consume them during the long winters. And it was used to make shrub—a combination of sugar, fruit, and vinegar that was imbibed straight, but also mixed with other beverages.

Hard cider also became political, especially in encouraging colonists to vote! Because colonists had to vote in county seats—and had to travel there—voting was often an all-day event, and by the time they got to the places where they would vote, they were thirsty. Enter in enterprising candidates, who would offer voters beverages to quaff their thirsts. George Washington, who initially resisted plying voters with booze in his first run for the Virginia House of Burgesses, decided to do the same in 1758, and besides rum, beer, and wine, his campaign manager also offered voters two gallons of cider royal. He won that election handily!

George Washington was a fan of hard cider, as were John Adams, Thomas Jefferson, and Benjamin Franklin. Hard cider was a staple of American troops during the war. In fact, during the Battle of Concorde an enterprising merchant named Elias Brown sold it to both revolutionary soldiers and the British during the lulls in fighting. During the American Revolution, it is believed that the Green Mountain Boys fueled up on a popular cocktail called the Stone Fence or Stone Wall (see page 138)—equal parts hard cider and hard liquor, often rum—before they captured Fort Ticonderoga.

Hard Cider Could Have Fueled Paul Revere's Famous Ride

Just about every elementary school child knows of Paul Revere's famous ride, shouting, "The British are coming! The British are coming!" But what is not taught is that before he became a famous craftsman and metalsmith, is that he once worked as a bartender. During his famous ride, he got the word out in the towns he visited by stopping at taverns, which were basically hubs of colonial life (you could drink, eat, stay at, and even mail your letters through taverns). Likely, folks at the taverns were drinking hard cider, beer, and rum (rum made in the Colonies by imported molasses was the most popular spirit at the time, but brandy, applejack, and whiskey were also imbibed), and Revere himself may have had a drink or two to quench his thirst on his ride.

Washington, in leading our troops, was also a leader in the consumption of booze: his Revolutionary War personal expense account for booze, from September 1775 to March 1776, amounted to more than $6,000. After the war and during his presidency, when his wife Martha and he would entertain, a typical dinner always included copious amounts of hard cider, beer, and wine. Though he never chopped down a cherry tree as legend holds it, he did plant 215 apple trees at Mount Vernon. His gardeners also grew pears, apricots, and, of course, cherry trees.

John Adams started every day with a giant glass of hard cider. He picked up the habit of drinking a "gill" of hard cider when he was a student at Harvard University, and he continued this habit for the rest of his life. He once wrote how "fresh and salubrious" enjoying hard cider was at the beginning of his day. Adams started his day by getting up before dawn, walking five miles and then drinking his hard cider, much as many people drink orange juice today. "It seems to do me good," Adams once wrote of his habitual drink. The only time he skipped his cider was when he was in Philadelphia, as he loved their beer. "I drink no cider but feast on

Philadelphia beer," he wrote in one letter to his wife Abigail. She made sure, during his presidency, that his house was filled with "favorite New England cheese, bacon, white potatoes, and cider." Adams believed that his good health could, in part, be attributed to consuming cider, and since he lived to be ninety, he might not have been wrong.

While it's widely known that our second president was a connoisseur of wine and attempted to grow grapes for making wine at his Monticello, Thomas Jefferson was more successful at growing apples. He, between 1767 and 1814, planted more than one thousand fruit trees, including eighteen varieties of apples, in Monticello's gardens. In fact, the gardens were so important to him that he had them planted before his stately house was even built. "I have known frost so severe as to kill the hiccory (sic) trees round about Monticello, and yet not injure the tender fruit blossoms then in bloom on the top and higher parts of the mountain," Jefferson wrote in his *Notes on the State of Virginia* in 1780. His hard cider apples included Hewe's crab apple and Taliaferro, and his favorite dessert apples were Newtown or Albemarle Pippins and Esopus Spitzenburg. Jefferson drank hard cider with the main course of his meals, as it was his "table drink," and he experimented with different blends of apples for his cider. The Hewe's crab apple, possibly a cross between a native crab apple and a European variety, was considered the most important apple and grown in Virginia at the time, but Jefferson's favorite was the Taliaferro, which he considered "the best cyder apple existing . . . nearer to the silky Champagne than any other." The Taliaferro, like many once popular apples, has disappeared.

It should be noted, however, that while Jefferson may have been the architect of his gardens, his actual plantation was run by slaves, and they were the ones who actually made the hard cider that he boasted about. Jupiter Evans, a slave who was Jefferson's personal valet among his many duties, also was in charge of bottling his hard cider. Evans was so good at cider making that when he passed away, Jefferson was in tizzy because his newer cider makers were bottling it too early, causing bottles to explode. When Jupiter died, Jefferson wrote "I am, sorry for him, as well as sensible he leaves a void in my administration which I cannot fill up." Today, a ciderie that's located nearby Monticello, Albemarle CiderWorks, has named its flagship cider in his honor. Jupiter's Legacy is made with a blend of 30 different apples.

Another of our founding fathers who was quite fond of hard cider was Benjamin Franklin. Among his many pithy sayings about cider: "He that drinks his cider alone, let him catch his horse alone," "It's indeed bad to eat apples; it's better to turn them all into cider," and "Give me yesterday's bread, this day's flesh, and last year's cider."

Johnny Appleseed, or Cider Goes West

Cider's popularity continued well into the nineteenth century. As settlers moved westward, so did the planting of apple orchards. And perhaps no planter was more famous than John Chapman, better known to kindergarteners everywhere as Johnny Appleseed.

But Johnny, as he came to be known, was not planting apples for munching. He was planting apples for cider making. Legends say he wandered barefoot with tin pan or pot for a hat and a sack of apples or seeds for planting. While the tin hat look isn't verifiable, he definitely carried apples and apple seeds everywhere in his travels.

He was born in the middle of the American Revolution, in 1774, and his father, Nathaniel, was a minuteman, serving under then-General Washington. His mother, Elizabeth, died less than two years later, giving birth to a brother. When his father returned from war, he married Lucy Cooley, and they had ten other children.

Little is known about John Chapman's early life. Some accounts say his father taught him farming and orcharding, others say he was apprenticed to another orchardist.

In any case, he eventually became quite accomplished at planting apple orchards, and at some point, he began traveling west. Some stories say he traveled to meet his family in Ohio, others say he traveled with his brother. But his westward walks were no idle meanderings. He traveled—and planted—with a purpose. Under frontier law, settlers could claim the land by establishing a homestead, and one way to accomplish this was to plant 50 trees. Johnny would plant orchards, later come back to tend them, and eventually, he would sell them to newer settlers coming west. He planted thousands of trees throughout Pennsylvania, Ohio, Indiana, and even Illinois. He seemingly had a gift to know where settlers were heading, and he got there first, planting trees. It's been said that, at one time, this entrepreneurial orchardist owned some 100,000 acres or so; for sure, by the time he died in 1845, he owned 1,200 acres, which his sister inherited (after settling taxes and debts).

Though he was quite the landowner, he was known for his eccentric habits. He dressed typically in used, sometimes threadbare, clothes, and he also often went barefoot. This may have been due to sacrifices for his faith, the Church of Swedenborg, also known as the New Church, for which he also evangelized. He never married, and he was known for his practice of abstinence. Because his beliefs were quite strident in respecting God's creation, he became a vegetarian in later life, respecting both the lives of people and animals, and several accounts say he wouldn't even hurt mosquitoes when they bit him. Johnny also did not believe in the process of grafting, as that would cause harm to the original trees. So, instead, he planted seeds.

Another thing that isn't taught in elementary school textbooks is that the trees he planted were definitely with the intention of drinking, not eating. Michael Pollan calls him an "American

Dionysus." In *Botany of Desire*, Pollan wrote, "From Chapman's vast planting of nameless cider apple seeds came some of the great American cultivars of the 19th century."

Johnny died in 1845 in Indiana, and that's really when his legend grew. Stories and books have been written about him, the US Postal Service issued a Johnny Appleseed stamp in 1966, and there's even a Johnny Appleseed Museum at Urbana University in Urbana, Ohio, not to mention several Johnny Appleseed festivals held across the country.

Howard Means examines how the man and the myth have mingled so much that it's hard to determine fact from fiction in his book, *Johnny Appleseed: The Man, The Myth, The American Story.*

Means points out that Chapman has been considered "the oddest character in all our history," but some people thought he was a saint. Others, though, "thought he had been kicked in the head by a horse." In any case, people just seemed to embrace him, wherever he went, and stories about him traveled across the land just like he did.

Today, at least one of his trees still stands, bearing fruit, in Savannah, Ohio, and descendants of the original farmers say Johnny stayed on the farm when he was in town, preferring to sleep in the corncrib rather than sleeping in the house.

The Zenith, then Fall, of Hard Cider

While Johnny's plantings of apple seeds proved popular, perhaps nothing denoted cider's stronghold on American culture more than the presidential campaign of former general William Henry "Tippecanoe" Harrison and John Tyler. While their Whig slogan of "Tippecanoe and Tyler too" might be remembered from high school history textbooks, the image they used to represent their campaign was a log cabin and cider barrel.

The symbols came from an article written by John de Ziska in a Baltimore newspaper, who believed that, at age sixty-seven,

Harrison was too old. He wrote: "Give him a barrel of hard cider, and settle a pension on him . . . he will sit the remainder of his days in his log cabin by the side of the fire and study moral philosophy!"

Harrison actually had enlarged a house which had a frame built around a log cabin, and he like so many people of the time enjoyed hard cider, likely made from apples cultivated on his own trees. As de Ziska intended his article to malign Harrison, Harrison and his party embraced the image. There was even a song and slogan written to embody this idea:

> They say he lived in a log cabin
> And lived on hard cider, too.
> Well, what if he did, I'm certain
> He's the hero of Tippecanoe.

Though the hero of Tippecanoe won the election, hard cider, it seems, was already on its way out. As the country expanded westward, the fertile lands of the Midwest were not only able to just support apple trees, but they were also climates that were better suited than the Eastern coast was to barley and hops, which waves of German immigrants took advantage of in making make quality beer.

These immigrants not only imported the recipes with them when they settled in the Midwest and Pennsylvania, but they also brought with them better beer-making techniques. Specifically, they knew how to make beer that didn't readily spoil. Unlike the very first beers made in the United States, besides the fact that they were sometimes made out of persimmons or cornstalks, they also were made with yeasts that fermented the beer on the top. These yeasts floated on top of the wort, and during brewing, they were exposed to the air. This not only made the beer attractive to bacteria and other yeasts within the brewing environment, they produced bad flavors and even worse, caused the beer to spoil. These hardworking brewmasters used bottom-fermenting yeasts—the yeasts stayed on the bottom during the process, so the resulting beers not only tasted better, they also weren't subject to spoilage.

Cider Press Innovations

Just as Harrison hailed from Ohio and Johnny planted those apple seeds in Ohio, Ohio was also home to an innovative inventor who figured there had to be an easier way of coaxing juice from pomace. W. G. Drucker developed the first hydraulic cider press in 1865, which revolutionized cider making. After the Civil War, he toured farms and demonstrated a working model. Demand for his press led to him founding the Mount Gilead Hydraulic Manufacturing Company in 1877, which manufactured presses for both large and small operations. Alas, today, the company (now known as HPM North American Corp.) no longer makes hydraulic presses for cider—its last big order was in World War II, when the Australian government needed twenty-four presses to manufacture cider for its troops.

Many of these German immigrants settled in cities, and cities were more conducive to brewing than cider making. Cider making had to occur in rural areas, where the apples were grown. Apples were too heavy to ship over great distances, and the shipping of apples over great distances also caused those apples to spoil. While apple transport was prohibitive, barley and hops could easily be shipped into cities, and thus, beer became more readily available in cities than cider. Americans also started migrating in larger numbers out of rural, cider-making areas and into cities, and along with urbanization, lager beer evolved into a much more preeminent drink.

Cider drinking was further diminished in the 1880s when some apple crops were so severely damaged by insects and disease. In fact, many apple trees were chopped down as a result.

Then along came the temperance movement. Temperance is often considered the biggest influence on cider's decline. Part of this is just the general demonization of alcohol—any and all alcohol was considered bad. But some nefarious cider makers did play a role in the demonization of alcohol. As the 1800s wore on, some cider makers increased the alcoholic content of their ciders by adding sugars to the juice before or during fermentation, and some of them even began adding hard liquor to their ciders. This wasn't just happening in the United States, it was also happening in England, and not only spirited things were poured in during the fermentation process. A "villainous compound of vinegar, glucose, whisky, and pepper" was added to some ciders, one article in 1890 expounded.

The temperance movement also really took hold in some rural areas, where another movement coincided and supported its goals, and that one is often called "the cult of domesticity." Catherine E. Beecher, the sister of Harriet Beecher Stowe, published *A Treatise on Domesticity*, in which she not only argued that a woman's sphere was that of the home, but she also advocated for no alcohol use within the home. "Wine is often useful as a medicine, under the direction of a physician, but its stimulating, alcohol principle makes it an improper agent to be drank in health. The same can be true of cider and strong beer." She believed that alcoholic beverages, except in use as medicine, were "never needful but as a general rule, are always injurious."

Some orchardists who were convinced by the temperance movement that cider was bad cut down their trees, and others created a pasteurized, unfermented juice called "sweet cider." This addition to our lexicon has confused people about the beverage ever since, and by 1900, Liberty Hyde Bailey wrote "the eating of the apple has come to be paramount."

In the early 1900s, part of cider's decline could also be traced to a federal law that prohibited the addition of preservatives of any kind in hard cider. This rule, of course, was backed by big breweries and other liquor producers.

The late 1800s and early 1900s also saw the proliferation of a new kind of fizzy competitor—soda. In 1876, root beer started being sold in larger numbers, and in 1881, the first cola-flavored syrup came on the market. Dr Pepper came out in 1885. Then, in 1886, Atlanta pharmacist Dr. John S. Pemberton created Coca-Cola. It also should be mentioned that Coca-Cola had a small amount of cocaine in its original recipe, and the drug stayed in the drink until 1928.

A good illustration of cider's decline before Prohibition is simply the statistics. In 1899, Americans guzzled 55 million gallons; by 1919, production had dropped to only 13 million gallons.

And just before Prohibition, an unusually cold Northeast winter killed some 1 million cider trees, and then after 1919, the trees started being culled in earnest, as federal agents axed cider trees throughout Prohibition.

Prohibition just about completely eliminated hard cider. The Volstead Act not only outlawed the sale of hard cider, it also limited the production of sweet cider to two hundred gallons per year per orchard. To survive, remaining orchards and nurseries cultivated sweet apples, which could be eaten. While breweries managed to stay afloat producing other goods, wineries stayed afloat producing sacramental wine and grape juice, and distilleries produced medicinal products, most cideries didn't have the same flexibility. Acres and acres of cider apple trees were burned or chopped down. Many heirloom cider apples dwindled away.

So, when Prohibition lifted in 1933, cider makers likely didn't have the right mix of apple cultivars to harvest for the traditional ciders people were used to. They also didn't have the flexibility to ramp up production when Prohibition was lifted in 1933. While most breweries could crank out beer, cideries would have had to replant trees, then cultivate these trees for at least five to ten years before apples could be harvested and fermented into cider.

While some cider trees escaped burning or cutting, they weren't cultivated with any intensity, and cider, as a beverage, disappeared.

Prohibition also changed our cultural vocabulary. Cider, by itself without any modifying adjectives, came to be known as that sweet, pasteurized juice. Juice producers dropped the sweet from their name, and cider, as an alcoholic beverage, came to be known as hard.

CHAPTER 3
The Apple Blossoms— or, Cider's Rebirth and Amazing Growth

"I'll squeeze the cider out of your Adam's apple."
—Moe Howard

THE RUIN OF APPLE TREES during Prohibition seemed to completely sound a death knell for America's rich and once flourishing cider industry. So much, that for much of the twentieth century, the term *cider* exclusively meant sweet, sappy apple juice.

While a few cider apple trees managed to survive the culling, sometimes as random survivors in the now-exclusively culinary orchards, for the most part, nobody was fermenting apples into hard cider in the United States for almost the whole of the twentieth century. Or at least, nobody was legally fermenting apples. As Angry Orchard head cider maker Ryan Burk said in an interview in 2017 of his native Williamson, New York, "I wouldn't want to give anyone's secrets away, but you could certainly find barrels of ciders fermenting in people's cellars . . . it's sort of something you knew about being from that town."

But unless you knew someone who was making cider in their cellar during this dark cider time, chances are, you probably had your first taste of cider if you traveled to one of the three cider-making regions of Europe (France, Spain, or England). Otherwise, you probably didn't know what cider was, much less that it had been the most American of all drinks. While in the 1970s and 1980s there were a few imported ciders on liquor store shelves, there really wasn't much traction in commercial cider making or cider drinking.

Things started changing in the 1990s. In 1990, hard cider production in the United States was at 750,000 gallons, according to Peter Mitchell, director of F&D Limited, in a cider report. Other sources say that it was much lower—somewhere around 250,000 gallons. In any case, it was way less than 1 million gallons. Or less than what many individual microbreweries might make in a typical year today!

But consider this: by 2004, according to Mitchell, Americans were consuming 4.25 million gallons, and by 2011, we were drinking 9.2 million gallons. By 2014, according to a white paper published by Tree Top, Inc., the production reached a whopping 52 million gallons.

An orchard worker harvests cider apples by hand.

Though production and valuation of cider as an entire industry has fluctuated up and down over the last five years, the overall growth is expected to continue, and while cider is still miniscule compared to beer and wine, its growth is staggering.

Perhaps the two most seminal cider houses to reintroduce cider to Americans were Woodchuck and Angry Orchard.

While plenty of traditional and even modern cider enthusiasts might look down on these producers since they use apple juice concentrate as an ingredient for many ciders, their contributions to the cider industry cannot be underestimated.

How Much Cider Can a Woodchuck Make?

Enough to change a country's drinking patterns. Greg Falling, who was a winemaker, decided that he should play around with some apples in his garage in Proctorsville, Vermont. He came up with Woodchuck Amber, using an old soda machine to fill the bottles. Since they only poured in 10 ounces, the last two ounces of every bottle had to be filled by hand with a turkey baster.

His experiment proved successful, and by 1996, his little company had produced 400,000 cases a year. Though the company sold first to Stroh's, then to Bulmer's (an English cider company that didn't quite understand the American market), by 2003 Bret Williams, Bulmer's first salesman, purchased the company, and by 2007, Woodchuck became the first cider maker to produce one million cases in a single year.

Cider Goes from HardCore to Angry

Boston Beer Company shook the cider industry up in 2012 when they retired their HardCore cider lineup and transformed it into Angry Orchard. According to industry reports at the time, they quietly launched the new cider brand, but it didn't stay quiet.

By 2014, they lured away cider maker Ryan Burk from Michigan, and in 2015, they opened a farmstead ciderie and orchard in New York.

"From a consumer perspective, the launch of Angry Orchard was a tipping point," says Eric West, cider expert and director of the Great Lakes International Cider & Perry Competition, the world's largest cider competition. "The product itself was not that different from other widely available brands such as Woodchuck, but Angry Orchard had the clout of the Boston Beer Company behind it."

Tracing Cider's Big "Little" Growth, or Where It's Going Now

While there were fewer than a dozen American cider makers in the early 1990s, today, according to IBISWorld, there are 959 cider makers, and by the time you're actually reading this sentence, there most likely will be more. Cider is made in forty-nine states; with a new cider maker starting in Wyoming, only Nevada does not have any in-state cider makers. According to Michelle McGrath, executive director of the United States Association of Cider Makers, in 2017 the US cider market was valued at $1.3 billion.

Over the last half of a decade, cider's experienced a rapid growth. "We were the fastest growing (alcoholic) category for three years running, and in a way, that got everybody excited about cider," says Paul Vander Heide, founder and owner of Vander Mill Cider in Grand Rapids, Michigan. "But we're still only one percent of the total beverage (categories) and only 2 percent of beer (category)." (It should be noted that although cider is NOT beer, its market share of alcohol is calculated within the beer category!)

According to IBISWorld, from 2013 to 2018, cider became the

fastsest growing alcoholic beverage industry in the United States. While cider consumption is still small compared to other alcoholic categories, growth is expected to continue to grow at an annual rate of about 20 percent, IBISWorld reports.

But doubling every year, for the industry, really isn't sustainable, Vander Heide says. So, one thing the industry did in 2013 was to actually form a formal organization, the United States Association of Cider Makers. "That was an important milestone," West says.

The USACM also formed a cider certification program—Certified Cider Professional—to educate servers, buyers, and distributors of cider. It's similar to certification programs for beer, wine, and cheese. The first certification level is Level 1 CCP, and then after passing that exam (which is online), the next level is Certified Pommelier™, which is like an advanced sommelier test and has to be administered in person. The very first exam was offered in Chicago in 2019 during CiderCon.

Education is key to growing more of a market share. "The first thing we try to tell people is forget what you think about drinking cider. Forget what you think you know, and revisit the category," Vander Heide says. "The most exciting thing we've got is such a direct tie to agriculture. It's so popular these days for people to get to know what they're eating or drinking and where it's coming from, and cider is one of the easiest beverages to tie back to its ingredients, right back to the ground the apples were grown from."

Looking at the sales numbers in 2017 can reveal some trends about where cider is going, McGrath points out. Of the $1.3 billion in sales, 75 percent of that was from national brands while 25 percent were from local or regional cideries. But 63 percent of those sales were on premises, which means they were at a cider house.

Off premises, cider growth is especially growing in cans (which also mimics the growth of craft beer and wine going into cans). "A big trend is for heritage cider makers to transition from 750 ml bottles into cans," McGrath says. "This is a big shift."

West says he sees slower or decelerating of growth by mass market brands, and faster growth by regional and local cider brands. "Consumer understanding and appreciation of cider will also continue to grow," he says.

Greg Hall, who spent twenty years as the brewmaster for Goose Island Brewing Company in Chicago before he opened Virtue Cider in Michigan in 2011, says the American market is ripe for growth. "We are still in the very early stages of cider in the United States," Hall says.

In Europe, the cider market makes up between 5 and 10 percent of the beer market. In England, it hovers around 17 percent, and in Australia, it's also between 5 and 10 percent. "While we may have had the lowest rate of cider consumption in the world, it won't be long until we drink more cider than everyone else in the world just because we're a big country, and people here like to drink just about everything," Hall says.

Hall predicts that the minimum overall growth of cider will be 5 percent of the beer market. "I think it's going to be a lot bigger than that," Hall says. "If you look at where beers are going, for a while, everyone's been made for IPAs, but I think cider will pass IPAs pretty quickly. I think cider can get to be between 5 and 10 percent of the market, bigger than most of Europe, but not quite as big of England."

The big reason Hall expects growth is the innovation of cider makers in the United States. A good way to take a look at American innovation is to consider the Great Lakes International

Cider & Perry Competition and its categories.

Way back in 2005, the first year Great Lakes International Cider & Perry Competition was held, there were only eight categories, plus a best of show. Last year, there were more than 1,000 entrants in 18 categories: modern cider dry, modern cider sweet, heritage cider dry, heritage cider sweet, traditional cider dry, traditional cider sweet, natural cider, modern perry, traditional perry, fruit cider, hopped cider, spiced cider, wood aged cider, specialty cider and perry, unlimited cider and perry, ice cider, fortified cider, and spirits. And in 2018, due to the exponential popularity of rosé in 2018, there's yet another category added to the contest.

"We have a very thirsty audience who wants to know what's new," Hall says.

In 2019, Virtue Cider will be debuting a new cider product called Mezzo Spritz. But instead of prosecco, it is cider-based, and instead of using a bitter liqueur like Campari or Aperol, it uses some blood orange and botanicals, topping it off with some sparkling water so that it has a very low ABV of 3.5 and only 80 calories. "You see so many bars with low-ABV cocktails," he says. "It ends up being really delicious on its own."

Another new product is debuting that is also similar to prosecco, but it's called Crispin Pearsecco. "There's no doubt that rosé has become wildy popular amongst cider drinkers," says Stephanie Zipp, associate marketing manager for Crispin. "Aside from that trend, pear flavors have been on the rise across the entire category. Crispin Pearsecco is a great example of a cider that incorporates pear notes."

Zipp notes that while cider drinkers as a whole are a diverse group of people, Crispin (along with plenty of other cider makers, it must be noted) is trying to get wine drinkers more introduced to the category. "Through in-depth research, our team has made a strategic decision to focus on targeting wine drinkers," she says.

"Our latest cider offerings drink like wine so we've had the unique opportunity to introduce wine drinkers to the cider category."

Cider drinkers aren't only interested in the latest developments—they are also thirsty for what's old, or for ciders made using older methods with actual cider apples, says Eleanor Leger, founder of Eden Specialty Cider in Newport, Vermont.

Of the cider renaissance that's been happening in the past decade, Leger says that the first wave was mass-produced ciders. The second phase was regional ciders made out of culinary apples, and now, people are discovering ciders made out of traditional cider apples. "Now there's a term for that—heritage ciders," says Leger. "There's more understanding and interest."

Cider needs to do a better job of defining itself and marketing itself, says Charlotte Shelton, owner of Albemarle Ciderworks & Vintage Virginia Apples in Virginia. "Cider has to be established as its own category," Shelton says. "It's not a wine. It's not beer. It has got to stand on its own legs and its own merits."

There's still work to do, Vander Heide says, but with the growth—especially in the categories of different ciders—he believes that more and more people will fall in love with this fermented apple beverage. "At our taproom, we have 26 to 28 ciders on draft," he says. "I usually feel pretty confident that we can take someone who drinks wine or beer or cocktails and find them a cider that they like. I think we're about 20 to 25 years behind where craft beer is."

CHAPTER 4
Apple Pickings: Things to Know to Better Enjoy Cider

"It was a beautiful, bright autumn day, with air like cider and
a sky so blue you could row in it."
—Diana Gabaldon

BY NOW YOU KNOW QUITE a bit about cider's history, and
if you're reading this book, you know you like to drink it. But to get
truly geeky about cider, let's get into the stuff that can enhance your
enjoyment.

The Glass Matters—and So Does the Temperature

While it's great on a hot summer's day to sip a cider out of a can or
bottle, the best way to enjoy it is to pour it into a glass.

And while any glass is better than just sipping it out of the
12-ml bottle or can you purchased it in, some glasses are better
than others.

The first is actual cider glasses. These glasses often look sort of
like a hybrid between wineglasses and beer glasses, but they're sort
of in the middle. And you don't have to search for them on Amazon—
you can actually get them at places like Williams-Sonoma, Home
Depot, and Bed Bath & Beyond.

Wineglasses can also work well. Whether they have stems or are
stemless, these glasses also concentrate the aromas of cider. Beer

glasses, especially for pilsners, can do the job, too. There are some basic categories of glasses that work well, but what they all have in common are fluted, bowl-like tops that concentrate the aromas.

Greg Hall, founder of Virtue Cider, says his favorite glasses for cider are stemmed Bordeaux glasses, and his second favorite are burgundy glasses. "The wine people have been doing this for a much longer period of time than the cider people," says Hall. "The Bordeaux glass has a nice bowl, but not quite as big of a bowl as the Burgundy glass, and it's got a nice, but not too big, entrance to the cider. That's my choice if I'm really going to enjoy a cider."

Jason Pratt, MillerCoors master cicerone (like a sommelier, but for beer) and senior marketing manager, says he prefers white-wine glasses for most ciders. "The shape of white-wine glasses does a great job of delivering the aromatic bouquet of the cider to your nose, and that can be the ideal glass for most ciders," he says.

But, Pratt says, red-wine glasses are better for bolder, higher ABV ciders. "Those ciders and ciders that are served a little warmer are better suited for glasses typically reserved for red wines where the wider bowl allows for greater surface area," he says.

The main thing that's important when choosing a glass is to select one made from a thinner material—the less of the glass, the better you'll enjoy the cider.

Temperature also matters. Most cider enthusiasts believe that cider is best enjoyed at a temperature somewhere around 50 to 55 degrees Fahrenheit. Simply take it out of the refrigerator, and let it sit at room temperature for about 5 to 10 minutes. For dryer, more tannic ciders, you may want to let the cider warm up even more.

While cider still tastes amazing even when it's ice cold, you're going to miss out on all of the different aromatics if it is too chilled.

That brings us to our next section—how to taste cider.

How to Taste

The basic procedure for tasting—and evaluating—cider can take its cues from wine and beer tastings. One of the best systems we've come across comes from Jaclyn Stuart, certified sommelier and owner of Vintage Elkhart Lake, a lovely boutique wine shop in Wisconsin. Stuart came up with a tasting system for wine called the

Eight S's of Wine Tasting. We're going to borrow it and call it the Eight S's of Cider Tasting.

See. Look at the cider. Note its color, hold it up to the light to see its clarity. Look at the bubbles.

Swirl. Gently hold the glass between your thumb and forefinger and rotate it a few times to swirl the cider around. Note, you don't want to create a tidal wave of force in or exploding out of your glass, but just gently swirl it around. This will help release the cider's aroma, and it will also create a little veil that may streak downward (especially if you're drinking a heritage cider). These drops or streaks are known as legs or tears. Because most ciders have lower ABVs than wines, ciders will have less legs than wines. But for some of the farmhouse ciders, with ABVs of 8 or 9, or ice ciders with higher alcohol content, you're definitely going to see more legs.

Sniff. Really put your nose right into the glass, and sniff. Your taste actually starts with your sense of smell, and in fact, if you open your lips just slightly while sniffing, you will draw more of the cider aromas onto your palate. Ask yourself: what does this cider smell like? Apples, yes, but how about apricots? Is it grassy? Or does it smell like a cat box?

Sip. Take just a little, tiny sip. Just enough to cover your palate.

Slurp. It's not rude—you are just aerating the cider more, and also involving more of your sense of smell in the process.

Swish. Move the cider across your tongue and all over your mouth. This way, all of your taste buds—sweet, sour, salty, bitter—will get covered. You don't have to gargle the cider, but you can pretend to "chew" it or drink as if you were actually eating solid food.

Swallow. Notice any lingering aromas and aftertastes, both good and bad. This is referred to as the cider's *finish*. As with wine, the longer and more enjoyable the finish, the finer the cider.

Savor. Think about the taste of the cider. How would you describe its flavor? Get your imagination involved. Does the flavor have a long or short finish? Was the cider balanced? What does its flavor remind you of? Did you like it or not? Why?

Big Words, but It All Comes Down to Flavor

This brings us to the various descriptions you can use to describe cider or the organoleptic terminology to evaluate cider. Organoleptic refers to the sensory evaluation of an alcoholic beverage, taking into account its appearance, taste, and flavors.

Part One: Start with a cider's appearance. Is it clear? Cloudy? Bright? Hazy? How big are its bubbles? What is its color? Light or dark, golden or amber, and is its color dark or pale? What is its consistency? Is it viscous, syrupy, or watery? What do its tears look like on the glass, and how long do they fall down the glass?

Part Two: Then, notice the cider's aromas. Aromas are where things can get more complicated.

If the aromas are unpleasant, they might smell vinegary, sour, or like solvents, fuel, or acetone. They might also smell oily or like plastic. They can even smell like rotten eggs or sulfury, rancid or soapy, catty or moldy. Obviously, these are all bad characteristics, but if something's off, you'll likely smell it right away.

Good aromas, on the other hand, are pleasant, and they can range from floral, fruity (and within fruity, outside of obvious apple or pear aromas, you can sense citrus, berry, currants, melons, etc.). They also might be grassy, earthy, caramel, toasty, nutty, or spicy. They can even smell sweet, but within the sweet notes, see if the cider is more like honey or molasses, sugar or artificial sweeteners.

Hall says that aromas can be broken down into three levels. The first set of aromas are of apple. All ciders have an appley aroma. But what you're going to want to do is focus on the kind of apple aroma. "We don't focus on the variety of apple because I don't really know anybody who can pick that out of a cider," Hall says. "Instead we focus on the type of apple."

There are three basic types: fresh, ripe, or overripe. "I think they're all not only acceptable aromas, but they're also all really great aromas," Hall says. And they're different. A fresh aroma is like the aroma of a freshly picked apple right off the tree, with perhaps just a note of skin or greenness or freshness.

A ripe aroma is an apple that is at its perfect point for eating—it's not gotten mushy or too soft, but it's lush and beautiful.

An overripe apple is an apple that's more than ripe; it's juicy, it could go bad so you'll either want to eat it or cook with it really soon.

Then after you notice the apple aromas, try and pick out the secondary fruit aromas. "Imagine these different aromas and how they translate into flavors," says John Enzenauer, head cider maker of Crispin. "I swirl slightly to help release the aromas and look for known smells."

Ciders can have citrus aromas like lemon or lemongrass, but they can also have tropical or banana scents, and they can also have some pear or cherry smells, too—and these are smells not just in flavored ciders, but in straight ciders without additions of other fruits or spices or herbs.

Then, the third level of aromas, Hall says, are the non-fruit smells. Think leather and farm, wood and toasted oak, mineral and vegetable. "It goes on and on," Hall says. "If you've got the right glass, take your time, going back and forth to smell the cider and pick up the different aromas."

"When I'm evaluating a cider, I ask myself, what do I smell, and is there anything there that does not belong?" says Enzenauer. "How is the balance of the cider—does one aroma overpower the others?"

While a certified Pommelier or sommelier or cicerone will likely be able to identify several

different flavors or aromas, it's okay if you only pick out one or two. The main thing is to use your imagination—what do you think a cider smells like? There's no one wrong or right answer.

Part Three: Taste, Mouthfeel, and Finish: After you note the aromas, the next thing you'll want to do is notice its taste, says Stephanie Zipp, associate marketing manager of Crispin. The taste can be crisp and sweet, clean apples or more baked apple-pie in taste, and you also might taste different fruits, spices, or herbs.

Enzenauer says that when you taste the cider, look at its sweetness, sourness, tartness, and bitterness. "Does it balance?" he says. "Is it too sweet or too sour?"

Aromas and taste go together, and taste also goes together with the consistency of the cider. When you taste the cider, notice its consistency on your tongue. Is it thick or light? Is it chalky or astringent? Creamy or warming? This consistency is called *mouthfeel*. "What is the viscosity?" Enzenauer says. "Is it light or heavy, and does it linger? Does it dry your mouth or wet your mouth? Once I go through this, then I just enjoy the cider for what it is intended: drinking."

The last part of evaluating a cider is determining what kind of **finish** it has. After you swallow the cider, do any flavors or aromas or sensations linger in your mouth? A good cider will have a finish. It could be tart, it could be tannic, it could be dry, it could be sweet . . . finishes are many different things, and like wines and beers, ciders have distinctive finishes that linger.

After you've sniffed and swirled and sipped and chewed a bunch of different ciders, you'll notice that every cider generally has a balance or imbalance of three properties: acids, sugars (or sweetness), and tannins, which are the chemical compounds found in fruit that cause a mouth puckering or dry and chalky feel. They're found in both ciders and wine, but they can also be found in coffee, tea, and chocolate. In some ciders, the acid level or acidity might be more than the sugars and tannins, or the sweetness might overpower the other two qualities. Some ciders have a little of all three while others have a lot of all three.

If you are doing a more formal evaluation of a cider or different ciders, you might want to keep a journal or a notebook in which you write down the cider's name, type, maker, and then your notes of what a cider tastes like. List the appearance, aromas, tastes, mouthfeel, and finish, and also note whether or not you like the cider and why or why not. That will not only give you a record of the different ciders you've tried, but you can also better figure out the styles, makers, and types of cider that you personally prefer.

Identifying Tannins

Tannins are the chemical compounds in both wine and cider that when the wine or cider ages, the tannins smooth out and mellow to create more complex flavors. But to more vividly understand what tannins are, think of two things: that mouthpuckering feel when you squeeze an over-steeped tea bag and sip those tea remnants. The second thing to think of or to try is to get a red grape and peel the skin back. Now, bite into that skin. That bitter, chalky dry feeling? Those are tannins.

Training Your Palate

Stuart says when she used to teach wine classes at restaurants and resorts, she would bring in things like currants, cherries, jams, etc.—the actual foods that different wines smelled like. You can do the same thing with cider—and if you're not sure where to start, look at the tasting notes on the bottle or the cider maker's website; they'll tell you if a certain cider has notes of honey or vanilla or oak or leather. Look at the notes, then make sure you have the different items a cider is supposed to smell like. Sniff the item—like freshly cut pears or bananas—then sniff the cider. That will train your nose to better pick out the different scents. You can also buy a sommelier's aroma kit—they're basically like small bottles of essential oils that smell like different things wine smells like. Stuart said that once she was in a grocery store in New York City, and she saw gooseberries on sale, and since some sauvignon blancs have notes of gooseberries, she purchased them, then got a bottle of wine with those aromas, and she was, from then on, much better at picking out gooseberry aromas in wines.

Cider Styles

Unlike wine sections both in liquor stores and on restaurant menus, unless you're in a cider-specific bar or store, ciders are just going to be kind of thrown together willy-nilly.

But to really understand the different ciders, let's take a few pages from the Great Lakes International Cider and Perry Competition style guidelines. While the categories within the competition grow every year—rosé ciders were just recently added—there are a few basic categories that remain the same.

The first is modern ciders. Modern ciders can be made directly from freshly pressed juices or apple concentrates or a combination. But they're mainly made almost exclusively from culinary apples. That means they're usually sweet, with higher acid levels and lower tannins levels. Their alcohol levels hover around 4 to 8 percent ABV, with most of the commercially made varieties rarely straying beyond a range from 4.5 to 5 percent.

Heritage ciders (sometimes known as farmhouse ciders) are made from many different kinds of apples, including cider-specific varieties like bitter sharps and bittersweets. They're higher in tannins, but they can range from dry to sweet, and their ABV ranges from 4 to 9 percent, but some can go much higher—11 to 14 percent. Some cider makers even use wild-grown apples and crab apples to press into cider—and these kinds are often funky, sometimes absolutely beautiful, and usually quite interesting.

Traditional ciders are those ciders made in France and England or by cider makers who use similar apple blends and ciders. They are both dry and sweet. English ciders have ABVs of 6 to 9 percent while French ciders range from 3 to 6 percent.

Natural ciders are Spanish-style ciders. They're fermented in different methods from French and English styles, and they're usually dry, with ABVs of 5 to 6.5 percent. More on all three of these regions in the next chapter.

It's also important to note that ciders can be aged in wood, mixed with herbs or spices, hopped up with hops, and/or combined with different fruits. If you don't like hops or if you do like sage, if you hate blueberries or love cranberries, then ciders flavored with various additions might or might not be to your liking. Flavored ciders can range in sweetness, from quite dry to very sweet.

The Order of a Cider Tasting

If you're tasting a bunch of different ciders, there are ways you can conduct a tasting to better enjoy and evaluate them. A good rule of thumb is to taste from dry to sweet, but end with the highest alcohol content ciders. Also, taste pure apple flavored ciders before you move into spiced or hopped or flavored ciders. And another tasting idea is to simply taste one category at a time—say, five sweet, apple-centric ciders or four dry rosé ciders or six ice ciders. If you stick to one category, and go from driest in that category to sweetest, you will get a lot out of your tasting.

Decoding Cider

(Or How to Figure Out If the Cider in Front of You Is Worth Drinking for Your Palate)

A lot of booze books list specific brands, whether it's cocktails, wines, or beers, but because liquor is regional, one type of whiskey that's widely available in Vermont isn't stocked anywhere at all in Arkansas, or a wine that's popular in Ohio isn't available in Montana.

Part of this is because so many wonderful craft breweries, wineries, distilleries, and cideries remain very small or very local. This remains especially true for ciders and distribution of ciders, as most of the nearly 1,000 cider makers in the country are solely local or regional producers, and they might only be distributed in the state where they're made, or, in some cases, only available in certain cities within certain states.

But even if it's not local, distribution of liquor varies wildly—because of leftover distribution laws from the post-Prohibition era and also because of liquor distributors, which vary from state to state. And unless it's a big international or national brand, finding space on shelves at liquor stores is also complicated. And even then, certain products are only available in certain places.

So, instead of listing very specific brands of cider that might not be available in your specific town or city or corner of the world, this chapter's going to reveal everything you need to know before you even sip a cider to determine whether you'll consider a cider worth your time. You'll be able to peruse a cider menu or scan the shelves at your local liquor store, and you'll be able to spot ciders you like.

The main problem most people have with ciders is it's such a big category, they don't know where to start. By now, if you've been reading this book in chronological order, you know the difference between a commercially produced cider and a heritage cider, but you might not be able to determine if you'll like a cider just by looking at a bottle or can.

A can of modern cider, made with apples grown in Texas, looks awfully similar to a can of commercially produced cider, made with fruit concentrates. A cider is not a cider is not a cider. So, what do you look at? Here are the visual cues—and words, phrases, and per-centages to look at.

Bottle or Can?

The first thing you'll see is whether the cider is in a bottle or a can, a 750 ml wine bottle, or a 12-ounce beer bottle.

If it's in a 750 ml wine bottle, that's the first clue that this kind of cider maker treats her or his cider like wine. Usually—*usually*—ciders in bottles are made by cider makers who also own or have access to orchards that grow cider apples. They might be flavored (they'll be labeled if they've got lavender or hops or cranberry or whatever), they might be aged in barrels (again, listed on the label), and they might even denote how many different varieties were pressed for the cider.

While cans are growing across all sectors of cider—and perhaps the fastest growing segment of cans are the heritage cider makers—this is often how you'll find commercially made cider: in 12-ounce cans or 12-ounce beer bottles.

A bigger, more commercial or more commercially-styled cider maker will list all of the ingredients and most likely will also list the calories and nutritional content. And this gets us to the most important part of cider detective work: reading the labels.

When cider drinkers say they like or dislike a specific cider, they're often talking about the sweetness of the cider, so the first thing you'll want to figure out is how sweet it is.

Most ciders, though, range from semisweet or semidry to off-dry and dry.

How Sweet It Is: Sweet or, Rather, Semisweet

Most commercial ciders range in the semisweet or semidry category. But calling a cider semidry really means, well, it's not dry, and therefore, it's sweet. While the category of sweetness is considered semisweet, most people would consider these ciders to be definitely sweet.

But within this candied category, there's a whole range of sweetness. So, how can you tell, just how sweet it is?

The first thing is to look at the ABV. Most ciders, as you've learned by now, fall in the 4 to 7 percent range, but a cider of 4.5 percent is definitely sweeter than a cider of 7 percent. So, first look at the ABV.

Second, read the ingredients listed. If it says no added sugars or no backsweeteners, then this is not going to be a supersweet cider. But things labeled as "lightly sweetened" sometimes are very sweet.

If there is sugar on the label—cane sugar, brown sugar, molasses, maple syrup, honey, corn syrup, fructose, etc.—there is some degree of backsweetening going on. The next step to determine just how sweet is to see where in the ingredients it is listed.

If the first ingredient is water, then fruit concentrates, then this is likely a sweeter cider, especially if sugars follow. If sugars come before water or cider, then this is going to be really sweet.

The other thing to look at is the nutritional content of the cider. Most nationally distributed ciders, whether they're made by a big company or even just a regional cider maker, will list the calories and nutritional content. The higher the calories in a cider, the more sugar it likely has. A cider with only 110 calories per serving is usually much lower in sugar than a cider with 250 calories per serving.

But the biggest thing to look at under nutrition is the sugars per serving. Some ciders have 0 sugars per serving, and those, as you might guess, are bone dry. Others, however have as many as

30 g per serving—that's almost a third more sugar than a serving of Chips Ahoy! cookies

Many have sugars of 10 to 15 g per serving (less than the 22 g per serving of a chocolate chip cookie!), but are not bone dry. That means, these ciders are sweet, but they aren't the sugar bombs a cider boasting 30 or close to 30 grams is. Depending on your personal sweet tooth, you might like some ciders more than others.

On the other hand, if the cider has 5 or less grams of sugar per serving, then it's a rather dry cider

Dry and Off Dry

Many dry ciders are labeled as such. Sometimes, they're still (and they're labeled as such), and often they're sparkling, but somewhere on the label, it will say dry. Some cider makers label their dry ciders as brut or brut reserve, but these are the ciders that no one would mistake for a wine cooler.

How dry they are can be from bone dry to medium dry or off dry. Unlike sparkling wines, which have specific labels for exact sugar levels, cider doesn't have such a system so you have to really look at the label to tell.

Another key to determining dryness is the overall ABV. While in general, many ciders boast an ABV around 5 to 7 percent, a good rule of thumb is the greater the ABV, the drier the cider. And within an individual cider maker's menu, you likely will see a range of ABV's—if one's 4.5 while the other is 5.7, then the one with the greater ABV is definitely going to be a bit drier.

And if it says on the label, an ABV of 11 or even 14 percent, then that's edging into red wine territory. Most red wines boast an ABV of 11 to 15 percent while white wines usually are 9 to 12 percent, and the drier the wine, the more alcohol (and thus, less sugar) the wine has. The same holds true for ciders.

They also sometimes list the exact ingredients. If they don't post a list of ingredients on the bottle, they might describe the cider as made from such-and-such apples, and if it contains any sugar or other backsweeteners, it might say "lightly sweetened," or if it doesn't, it might say something like "no additional sugars added."

Other Words to Look for

Now, you likely can look at a can or a bottle and make a pretty good guestimate of how sweet the cider is and whether you'll like that level. And if you are like many people, chances are, you might like a range of sweetness, depending on the circumstances of your cider drinking. You might like a bone dry cider for an elegant seafood dinner, but you might really appreciate a sweet, blackberry cider if you've just finished mowing the lawn on a very hot summer day. Or, you might really love a modern cider of a 4.5 percent ABV, but with no backsweeteners, to sip at a tailgating party.

That said, there are some other terms to look for on a label.

Unfiltered means that the cider's not going to be crystal clear—it might be slightly cloudy, or there may or may not be some sediment.

Unpasteurized means that the local, wild yeasts were allowed to work with the yeasts the cider maker added. That could mean a funkier cider, or, it just means that it's a little more interesting than a typical, commercially produced cider.

Wild fermentation means, well, the cider was allowed to get wild at some point, and the fermentation period likely was a lot longer than the days or weeks of most ciders.

Barrel-aged means that the cider has been aged, and if it's been labeled and dated, then treat it as a wine that has been aged. This is going to be a much more interesting cider than many.

If the cider's labeled as **tannic** or **aged**, then, again, this is going to be a more complex cider. Look at any types of apples that are listed on the labels, whether it is a single varietal (quite intriguing, as most ciders are blends), and whether it is mostly culinary, or a blend of culinary and cider, or just cider apples. If they are mostly culinary apples, then the cider is most likely going to be sweeter and more acidic than tannic, and it will not be as complex as ciders made with cider apples or a blend. And if it says **wild apples**, then it could be very, very interesting (some wild apple blends are out-of-this-world, crazy good, and others are merely interesting).

Ice and Dessert Ciders

Ciders range in sweetness from super-duper sweet to bone dry, but if we're talking ice ciders or dessert ciders, these ciders are in a category all their own because of sweetness and because of the very, very careful way that they are made. These babies have a residual sugar amount that can range from 4 percent to a whopping 15 percent, and their ABV is usually 10 percent or greater. They're delicious, typically expensive, and they come in thin little bottles just like ice wines and dessert wines. They're rarer than most other types of ciders because they take such a long time to make, and to make them naturally (without putting the apples in the freezer), they have to be cultivated in the very northern apple regions. They originate in Quebec, but northern Vermont, Michigan, and Wisconsin are some of the places that make ice ciders.

More Cider Detective Ideas

The more you get to know your own taste buds, the better you'll know if you like a cider or not. But, you also probably have some friends who have similar palates to yours. If your friends or family members like certain things that you know you'll like, then ask them.

Test Your Detective Work

A good way to see if you understand how to read cider labels and containers is to set up a taste test at home. Pick about three to five ciders, but no more than eight—you don't want to overwhelm your taste buds yet you want a good sampling for comparisons.

Study the labels and containers, and then, write down your pre-impressions of each cider. Do you think it will be sweet or dry? How sweet or how dry? Other flavor or aroma ideas? Then, line the ciders up, from what you think will be the driest to what you think will be the sweetest. Then, taste and take notes.

How did your actual tastes of the ciders match up to your preconceived notions of the ciders? Were you spot on, or were things not quite how you imagined them to be? If they weren't quite spot on, why? What factors do you think changed the actual tastes from your impressions? Note those.

But the other thing is to figure out what you like. Sweet or dry or in between? Fruit-flavored additions or botanical additions? Tannic or not?

And if you want to get up-to-the-minute reviews, one app you might want to install onto your phone is Cider Expert. It's the only cider reviews-based app that keeps track of your preferences (some beer review apps also keep track of ciders, but they're not exclusively cider-based).

It's not a perfect app, but you can look up a cider brand and name of a specific cider, and then you can read reviews other people have listed, and you can also review ciders yourself and keep track of all the ciders you've tasted.

It has a range for things like sweetness, sparkling, bitterness, and funkiness, but the levels of sweetness, especially, aren't clear-cut, and you'll have mass-produced ciders listed as having the same levels of sweetness as some heritage ciders, and if you look at the ABVs of those ciders, their sweetness levels should be markedly different.

Still, it is a way to keep track of ciders, and by reading the reviews, you can tend to see if someone has taste buds that are similar to your own.

Another service you might want to try is a cider subscription. While one of the best things you can do is join a cider club from one of your favorite cider makers that you've visited, not a lot of individual cider makers have cider clubs the way wineries have wine clubs. We expect that will change as ciders grow in popularity.

In the meantime, there is one heritage cider subscription business called Cider In Love (ciderinlove.com), which is an "online curator" of heritage ciders. They connect heritage cider makers through their website, and make it easy for cider lovers to shop for them. The way it works is you buy directly from the cider makers themselves (they pay the website a small marketing fee, according to CIL). Besides streamlining online cider shopping, the site also offers fun stuff like matching individual ciders to styles of wine, cider recipes, and tasting notes.

While this new website is innovative in and of itself, and it does have some drawbacks, mainly, the limited geography of the cider makers themselves—only cider makers fermenting in the northwest, New England, New York, and California are included, and that leaves out giant swaths of cider makers in the middle of the country and in the south, and the terroir of these cider makers, not to mention the apples themselves, are very different. This is disappointing, but perhaps if CIL is successful, they'll branch out to include other notable cider makers in their collection.

CHAPTER 5
Apple Travels and Apple Fun

"Everybody thinks I drink beer, but I actually like cider!"
—Prince William

To TRULY UNDERSTAND CIDER, you should travel to places where cider is made or where cider is curated and served. Fortunately, 49 states and the District of Columbia boast cider makers. The only state that doesn't yet have a cider maker is Nevada, and even there, you'll find some taprooms and bars that offer decent collections of cider (and perhaps, by now, Nevada might have a burgeoning cider maker in its midst).

Ciders aging in barrels in Basque Country, Spain.

Tasting cider at a cider maker is like tasting wine at a winery or touring a craft brewery. You won't truly understand the process unless you're actually right there, smelling the ferment of apples, seeing the tanks and hoses, and viscerally experiencing how such a glorious beverage is made. While not every cider maker might make a style you prefer, when you visit a cider maker, you get to taste things that may not be distributed outside of the orchard or tasting room, and you can get up close and personal with cider in a way that you can't experience elsewhere.

And fortunately, no matter where you live in the United States (or Canada, for that matter), there likely is a cider maker, or at least a pub or taproom that knows cider, near you.

According to the United States Association of Cider Makers, 64 percent of cider sales in 2017 were on premise, meaning that cider makers sold them from their own farms, tasting rooms, or cider houses. The United States has more than nine hundred cider makers, and the numbers keep growing. That's a lot of cider. The five biggest producers of cider are New York, Michigan, California, Washington, and Oregon.

"Except for California, which is an agricultural state, all of those regions are apple states," says Michelle McGrath, executive director of the association. And while those top states have dozens upon dozens of cider makers, plenty of other states have way more than a dozen makers, including Virginia, Vermont, Pennsylvania, Ohio, Colorado, Wisconsin, Massachusetts, and North Carolina. Other places are doing some interesting things with cider, including New Jersey, where there's a researcher at Rutgers University who is testing cider apples to help revive the state industry (New Jersey once produced the "champagne" of ciders in the United States).

The easiest way to experience cider is to find the closest cider maker to where you live. And you can find such cider makers the old-fashioned way and Google cider near your location, or you can go straight to three online resources that have curated the cider makers for you. All three websites offer different resources and calculate cider makers differently so you might want to check all three, especially if you live somewhere there's only one or two makers near you.

The first website is the United States Association of Cider Makers, ciderassociation.org, where there is a *Find a Cidery* search button you can click, and then you can input a name, state, US territory, or Canadian province to find local cideries and their websites (it's the only website where we found a cidery in Puerto Rico).

CiderGuide.com, published by cider expert Eric West, is also a great reference, and he has an interactive map you can click on and cider makers pop up. He has cider maps of the United States, Canada, and the world that also give you an idea of where you might travel for cider. He does list a disclaimer, though, saying that the world of cider has grown so fast, his map is more of a historical reference than an in-time collation of current producers. He also has, in the past, published a newsletter and podcast on cider, and his website lists festivals, cider books, and lots of other information that can get you started when you think about traveling and cider.

The other really excellent site to find a cider maker is Cydermarket.com. What's really nice about this website is that twice a year, it reviews all site links to cider makers, books, cider equipment, festivals, etc. With this maintenance work, the site also updates its USA Cider Makers Database, and in doing so, they note the growth and change in the industry. The site can help you locate places to buy local cider as well, and this is also the only online site that curates cider pubs and restaurants by geographical location, too.

Cider Festivals and Cider Weeks

Anywhere there is a concentration of cider makers, there's a Cider Week or Cider Festival or some cider-related event. Perhaps the biggest cider event of them all is CiderCon, which is hosted annually by the United States Association of Cider Makers.

CiderCon is a week's worth of cider tastings, classes, and networking. It's for cider makers, but cider enthusiasts are also welcome. This is where you'll really discover cider styles, places, and makers.

After CiderCon, the biggest event is Cider Summit (cidersummitnw.com). It's held in Chicago, San Francisco, Portland, and Seattle, and every summit is regional in nature. It's a one-day event, featuring cider makers from all over the world, but every summit is a little bit different and features a different smattering of makers and tastings. Often, local cider weeks happen the week the summit comes to town. You can also volunteer for Cider Summit, but those positions fill up pretty fast.

At the Great Lakes International Cider and Perry Competition, held in Grand Rapids, Michigan, you can also volunteer, but you need actual experience and expertise to be tapped as a volunteer. The competition also coincides with Cider Week GR. There are also Cider Weeks in New York City, Virginia, Oregon, Montana, Vermont, Washington, Western New York, Philadelphia, Minnesota, Quebec, and more. There are also smaller Cider Weeks and cider tastings in cities like Washington, D.C., Toronto, and Milwaukee. CiderGuide.com lists cider festivals by date and location, and it's a pretty good compilation of events.

Cider Abroad

If you're planning a trip abroad somewhere, why not sample some of the local cider culture while you're traveling? Dozens of countries boast local cideries, pubs, and even tasting routes, but outside of the United States, the absolute biggest are the United Kingdom,

Spain, and France, which, as you know, historically, developed the cider-making traditions and apples used even today. And,
you can't forget Canada, either, because you
can find a cider maker in eight different
provinces, and cider-making traditions,
especially in Quebec, run deep.

But let's start with the United Kingdom,
where nearly half of all cider in the world is
consumed.

United Kingdom of Cider

By volume, the fine citizens of the United Kingdom consume more
cider and make more cider than anywhere else in the world, and no
matter where you go, you'll find cider served. You can buy it in cans
from a corner grocery store, get it on tap at a pub, or sip it at a sports
event. Some of the world's biggest cider makers make their homes
here, but so too do some of the most intricate and small farmhouse
makers.

Within the UK, there's a great debate over what should be called
cider, and at the forefront of that discussion is the Campaign for
Real Ale (CAMRA), which says that that cider should only be rightfully called cider if it's entirely natural, meaning noncarbonated,
unpasteurized, and made strictly from freshly pressed apples (no
concentrates whatsoever). On the other end of the spectrum are
large corporations, which make very sugary and either watered-
down or alcohol-enhanced types of cider, and in the middle are
modern cider makers who might use freshly pressed juice, but also
enhance carbonation or filter their ciders, etc. Whole books could
be dedicated to this subject, but just know that there are extremes
in cider when it comes to the UK.

To get your start in exploring cider on the isle, a good clear-
inghouse is real-cider.co.uk. Not only does it list makers by website
(and warns that some of the smaller ones may not accept regular
visitors), but it also includes a link to festivals and events by date
and location.

Within the UK, you'll find the largest concentration of cider makers in the following areas: Somerset, Devon, Worcestershire, Gloucestershire, and Herefordshire. Herefordshire produces the most cider in the country, which it has been doing since the end of the seventeenth century. Herefordshire is home to both giant cider producers and small farmhouse producers.

Good English ciders are, of course, made with cider apples, but the mix of cider apples in England leans heavily on more tannic apples, though the exact blend of cider apples varies from region to region.

To figure out which cider houses to visit, VisitBritain.com and TheCultureTrip.com detail different makers and orchards that offer tours and tastings.

The World of Sidra in Spain

While the United Kingdom might drink more cider by volume, in the regions where *sidra* (cider) is produced in Spain, more cider is consumed per capita. In the UK, people drink cider alongside ales and wines, but if you go to Asturias in Spain, the locals *only* drink sidra, completely ignoring the fine wines and beers made elsewhere in the country.

The two main regions of sidra in Spain are Asturias and Basque Country. Asturias, in fact, is called the *Comarca de las Sidra* or Cider Region, and here is where there is an official Apple and Cider Route, with guided tours, a Cider Museum, and restaurants with cider tasting meals. You can find information about Asturias at Spain.info or LaComarcadelaSidra .com.

Asturias has not only the makers of cider and the orchards, but it's also got an incredible amount of *sidrerias*, or cider bars. And the experience at a Spanish cider bar is like no other. The main reason for that is because they have a cider-making and cider-throwing tradition that goes back two thousand years.

It's an art to behold an *escanciador*, or server, who tilts the bottle of cider for you and throws the cider through the air into a glass, which temporarily carbonates the cider, giving it a mousse-like consistency.

In Basque Country, there's also a cider route, and the tradition is a bit different than in Asturias. The sidra here is a bit more tart and not at all sweet, and it's served directly out of barrels. Astigarraga is the official cider capital of Basque Country, and tourists come out by the busload, from January until April, to enjoy all the sidra you can drink at the cider bars. A good source of information is En.TravelBasqueCountry.com.

Sidra is also served at bars and restaurants throughout the entire country of Spain, and there are several cider bars within its capital city of Madrid.

Cidre, or Fine French Cider

Cider making in France is concentrated in Normandy and Brittany, the northwest regions of France (just like the cider making is concentrated in the northwest regions of Spain). By volume, after United Kingdom, France consumes the next largest amount of cider in Europe, and no wonder—its effervescent *cidre* is amazing.

In Normandy, En.Normandie-tourisme.fr., you'll find an official cider route that links up twenty different producers of cider and calvados. It's located to the east of Caen, linking up Beuvron en Auge, Bonnesbosq, Beaufour, and Druval, through beautiful, lush countrysides and orchards.

Brittany, while less well known than Normandy, also produces cider from only seven varieties of apples that have to be harvested by hand. Cornouaille is the center of Brittany cider. Check out Finisterebrittany.com.

The label *cidre doux* means sweet cider while *demi-sec* is semi-sweet, and *cidre brut* is very dry. There's also calvados or fine brandy to taste and pommeau, an aperitif made by blending brandy with fresh apple juice that's aged. And if it's labeled *poire*, that means it's perry.

Canadian Cider

Settlers from both England and France brought with them their cider-making traditions. Though Canada has a bit colder climate than many cider-making regions, apples obviously grow there, and there are eight different provinces that make cider. Wines of Canada (WinesofCanada.com) has a listing of cider producers, organized by province, and they do update their listings. CyderMarket.com and CiderGuide.com also list Canadian producers.

The biggest regions for cider are near Canadian regions for wine, including Quebec, Ontario, British Columbia, and Nova Scotia. There are more than 100 different Canadian cider producers. Though Canada did enact a Prohibition of alcoholic beverages, it was only from 1918 to 1920, and unlike in the United States, cider orchards were not burned or cut down, but similarly to what happened in the United States, cider fell out of favor as beer grew in popularity. As such, cider apples were not cultivated much, and culinary apples rose in stature.

In Canada, the cider revival really started in the 1970s, after the Quebec Liquor Commission (which had been established in 1921), added cider back into the list of allowed products (for some reason, it was left off the original list), and cider started being produced.

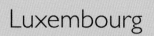

Luxembourg

While France, Spain, and the United Kingdom get most of the European attention for cider making, other areas of Europe also make cider. Perhaps the newest comer to commercial cider making in Europe is Luxembourg.

Luxembourg, a tiny nation with less landmass than the state of Rhode Island, has had a bit of a cider renaissance since Carlo Hein founded Ramborn Cider in 2015. While Luxembourgians made and drank cider, it was not a commercial enterprise, and Hein founded it, in part, because he kept seeing apple orchards die off.

Ramborn Cider in Luxembourg. Photo courtesy of Ramborn.

The small Ramborn Cider Haff (house) in Bern, Luxembourg, offers tours of its orchards, its cider-making facility, as well as its tasting room. Ramborn.com details more of the experience.

It really took off after Christian Barthomeuf created the very first ice cider, or *cidre de glace* in 1989. It was modeled after the ice wines, which are made in the fall and winter, when the fruit is heavy with sugar and freezes outside. And pretty much all of the 60 or so cider makers in Quebec now make at least one ice cider. CidreduQuebec.com is a great resource to find cider houses in Quebec.

The cider regions of British Columbia, Nova Scotia, and Ontario started cultivating and crafting ciders in the early 2000s, and today, cider making continues to grow. For more information, you can also visit OntarioCraftCider.com to find out where to visit cider makers in Ontario, and for information about British Columbia cider makers, check out the British Columbia page of the Northwest Cider Association NWCider.com (this website is also great if you're planning to visit any of the cideries in the northwestern states in the United States). For Nova Scotia, check out TasteofNovaScotia.com to see the most up-to-date listing of cider makers.

Cider in Literature

Daniel Dafoe wrote a little bit about cider. Ben Franklin did, too.

Washington Irving was a journalist and some even considered him a food critic, before he wrote about the pumpkin-headed ghost in *The Legend of Sleepy Hollow*.

A ripe Luxembourgian apple at harvesttime.

In a letter he wrote in 1807, Irving waxes a bit poetic about things, including cider. "The people, in fact, seem to be somewhat conscious of this propensity to talk, by which they are characterized, and have a favorite proverb on the subject, 'all talk and no cider;' this is particularly applied when their congress, or assembly of all the sage chatterers of the nation, have chattered through a whole session, in a time of great peril and momentous event, and have done nothing but exhibit the length of their tongues and the emptiness of their heads."

While most folks know about the headless horseman and Ichabod Crane in *Sleepy Hollow*, they might not realize that hard cider and the apples it is derived from both make an appearance. As Crane makes his way to the dinner party where he will see Katrina, the young woman he's been pining over, he waxes poetic over the "orchards burdened with ruddy fruit."

Characters casually "take a hearty draught of cider" in some of James Fenimore Cooper's novels, Louisa May Alcott wrote about "cider applesauce" in a short story called *An Old-Fashioned Thanksgiving*, and Mark Twain once wrote, "I know the look of an apple that is roasting and sizzling on the hearth on a winter's evening, and I know the comfort that comes of eating it hot, along with some sugar and a drench of cream . . . I know how the nuts taken in conjunction with winter apples, cider, and doughnuts, make old people's tales and old jokes sound fresh and crisp and enchanting."

And while Stephen Crane was famous for his book *The Red Badge of Courage*, he once wrote a letter to the editor: "To the Editor: What can I do with my voice?" "In the spring, Stephen, you can plough with it, but after corn ripens, you will have to seek employment in the blue-stone works. We have seen voices like yours used very effectively as cider-presses."

One of the most romantic description of cider comes in Nathaniel Hawthorne's 1860 novel, *The Marble Faun or The Romance of Monte Beni*. This romance is set in Italy, where Hawthorne contrasts the wine making of the country with the cider making of New England. "New England vintages, where the big piles of golden and rosy apples lie under the orchard trees, in the mild, autumnal sunshine; and the creaking cider-mill, set in motion by a circumgyratory horse, is all a-gush with the luscious juice."

But perhaps the loveliest writing on cider comes from Henry David Thoreau, who penned an essay called *Wild Apples*. This descriptive work was published posthumously in 1862 in *The Atlantic Monthly*. In this piece, Thoreau expounds upon the history, beauty, and meaning of both apples and apple trees, but especially of wild apples. He mourns the rise of temperance and the growth of grafted apples, saying that the days of the wild apple were numbered:

> The era of the Wild Apple will soon be past. It is a fruit which will probably become extinct in New England. You may still wander through old orchards of native fruit of great extent, which for the most part went to the cider-mill, now all gone to decay. I have heard of an orchard in a distant town, on the side of a hill, where the apples rolled down and lay four feet deep against a wall on the lower side, and this the owner cut down for fear they should be made into cider. Since the temperance reform and the general introduction of grafted fruit, no native apple-trees, such as I see everywhere in deserted pastures, and where the woods have grown up around them, are set out. I fear that he who walks over these fields a century hence will not

know the pleasure of knocking off wild apples. Ah, poor man, there are many pleasures which he will not know! Notwithstanding the prevalence of the Baldwin and the Porter, I doubt if so extensive orchards are set out to-day in my town as there were a century ago, when those vast straggling cider-orchards were planted, when men both ate and drank apples, when the pomace-heap was the only nursery, and trees cost nothing but the trouble of setting them out. Men could afford then to stick a tree by every wall-side and let it take its chances. I see nobody planting trees to-day in such out-of-the-way places, along the lonely roads and lanes, and at the bottom of dells in the wood. Now that they have grafted trees, and pay a price for them, they collect them into a plat by their houses, and fence them in—and the end of it all will be that we shall be compelled to look for our apples in a barrel.

As illustrated above, with the exception of Thoreau's essay, much of hard cider's appearances in great works of literature are in passing. It was just a beverage that people drank, and it was everywhere so it wasn't so much a plot point or a special feature, it just was.

Now, twentieth-century and twenty-first-century authors are taking cider as a setting or mention in a novel wider and farther, and there are whole novels dedicated to hard cider. Here's a short selection of cider books to add to your nightstand.

The Simplicity of Cider: A Novel, by Amy E. Reichert, portrays a gifted but prickly cider maker whose life is upended when a man and his boy show up at her family's orchard.

Hard Cider Abbey: A Barefoot Monk Mystery, by K. P. Cecala, weaves a quirky tale about a silent monk who investigates the murder of the monastery librarian in Appalachian West Virginia.

Hard Cider Lessons by Barbar Stark Nemon, tells the story of a woman who is working to realize her dream of producing hard cider on the northern banks of Lake Michigan.

The Cider House Rules, by John Irving, doesn't revolve around hard cider, but the title comes from a listing of regulations inside a cider house and posted by a light switch.

Cider with Rosie, by Laurie Lee, is the first book of a memoir trilogy of Lee's childhood in Gloucestershire. Like *The Cider House Rules*, it was made into a movie.

Cider in the Movies

Besides *The Cider House Rules* and *Cider with Rosie*, there are a few films that make mention of hard cider.

Little Brown Jug is an animated short directed by Seymour Kneitel and Orestes Calpini in 1948, and hard cider and farm animals take the center stage. This Paramount audience-participation, follow-the-bouncing-ball singalong tells of what happens after too many apples get blown off a tree and an old cider mill breaks down from the overload. Basically, all the animals get inebriated, with things like a cow giving 100-proof milk.

More recently, hard cider shows up as a plot point in *Fantastic Mr. Fox*. There's a secret cider cellar in Mr. Bean's farm, and Mr. Fox breaks into the secret cider cellar. The movie is actually based on a Roald Dahl children's book of the same name, published in London in 1970, but the fantastic plot holds up quite well with time.

In both the Broadway play and movie *Guys and Dolls*, the main character Sky Masterson shares some advice his father relayed to him: "One of these days in your travels, a guy is going to come to you and show you a nice, brand-new deck of cards on which the seal has not yet been broken. This man is going to offer to bet you that he can make the jack of spades jump out of that deck and squirt cider in your ear. Now son, you do not take this bet, for as sure as you stand there, you are going to wind up with an earful of cider."

It's not quite "Riunite on Ice—That's Nice" memorable, but hard cider makers are promoting their beverages on television with humor, and some are even getting recognized by the advertising community. A 2016 commercial for Strongbow, featuring Patrick Stewart, starts out with a narrator voicing that the company had hired an award-winning actor to promote their lineup of ciders, but she canceled. Stewart, indignant and outraged tries to relay that he's received thirty-seven individual awards, but then the narrator cuts in and says "Yeah, but for acting. STRONGBOW!"

CHAPTER 6
Crushed—or, a Simple Cider Recipe, plus Techniques and Tips

"Never praise your cider or your horse."
—Benjamin Franklin

So, you've tasted your way through your favorite cider bar, got your local liquor store to bring in new ciders from across the country, or visited several cider houses on vacation. You're so buzzed about cider (pun intended) that you really want to try your hand at making your own. After all, how hard can it be—it's just fermented apple juice, and people have been making it for centuries, right?

Well, cider making can be both simple and complex, but with a little know-how and some definite forethought, you can make a delicious hard cider that you can take to your next neighborhood block party, family gathering, or celebration and be proud to share it.

To guide you through the home cider-making process, we tapped two experts. The first expert is Jessica Shabatura. Shabatura loves to make both hard cider and wine in her Arkansas home. She loves plants and fermentation so much that she was inspired to get her bachelor's of science in horticulture.

Shabatura's father is a food scientist so she grew up loving chemistry (and playing with her food). She's tried to make wine out of just about anything—including produce going bad (which kinda works) and Frosted Flakes (which doesn't work at all). "The preservatives in the cereal killed my yeast," she says.

But more importantly, Shabatura created the excellent, go-to website for all things about making hard cider at home, aptly named www.howtomakehardcider.com. Here, she's detailed her experiments with all things apples, fermentation, and juice, and she's helped hundreds of people who've emailed her after their very first attempts at making hard cider have failed.

Our second expert is Walker Fanning. Fanning is the owner of Hidden Cave Cidery in Madison, Wisconsin. An agronomy major at the University of Wisconsin, he was studying large-scale farming, focused on big grains like corn and wheat, but he always wanted to get into specialty crops. The summer after he graduated, he tried to find a job at local wineries, but they were doing barely any hiring, so he decided that maybe he should volunteer to work at an apple farm.

So, he took a map from the Wisconsin Apple Growers Association, then did a search for farms with value-added products like hard cider within a short distance from Madison. He found one, called up the farmer, and said, "I have a farming background, and I'm interested in learning about your orchard." He got the job of orchard manager, and he not only managed the small orchard, but he also started selling the apples and hard cider.

"The first time I tasted the cider, it blew my mind," he says. "But then, the next batch of cider tasted like thin, apple water. It tasted completely different. I told (the owner), 'I can't sell this—it's completely different from the cider your customers are expecting.' He said 'Well, this is what we have, what can we do?'"

Fanning ended up revamping this little orchard's cider-making process to ensure that they always sold a consistent product, and he marketed it to local bars and restaurants around Madison. When he started, the cider was only sold in two locations, but by the time he left, it was distributed to thirty places. While working for this cider house, Fanning learned his craft, but he always knew he one day wanted to open his own cidery. At a local meeting of the Madison Beverage Makers Group, he met Nathan Greenawalt, owner of Old Sugar Distillery, who had just received his winemaking permits from the state. Fanning ended up working for Old Sugar, and within Old Sugar's Madison-based distillery, he founded Hidden Cave Cidery in 2018.

Anyone can make hard cider, and actually, anyone in all fifty states can *legally* make hard cider. So long as you are at least twenty-one years of age, and as long as you're not selling the hard cider (uh, moonshine cider, anyone?), you can legally make up to 100 gallons of hard cider in your home. Any quantities greater than that—and that makes 540 12-ounce bottles—and you'll run afoul of the law. And need permits and licenses. And if you don't have the permits or the licenses—and you get caught—you could get arrested.

And let's face it, if you've made that much cider (which equals 90 six-packs), maybe you should go into business legally.

Starting Out: Go Small

For your very first batch of cider, it's easy to get excited and get carried away and suddenly, you're making gallons and gallons and experimenting with recipes . . . and then, then you fail. One of the main things Shabatura emphasizes with every hard-cider-making newbie is to start small.

We'll say it again. Start small.

Though making hard cider is not rocket science, like all fermented products, you make it, and then you have to wait out the fermentation process to see if what you've made actually tastes good. And, if for your very first venture into cider making, you make a batch of blech, well, you might not be inspired or determined enough to ever go through that time-consuming process again.

"It's worse than going out and buying a bottle of wine and dropping it in the parking lot," Shabatura says.

"You want to hit undo, but there's no getting it back. And you're not just looking at this shattered bottle, you now have a tub of stuff that's just disgusting. It literally tastes like gym socks, it's that horrible, and this time, you've now wasted all this time."

Not to mention money and resources. If you've made 10 or 20 gallons that are undrinkable, then, well, you've wasted money on all that juice, yeast, and anything else you put into it. And you have absolutely nothing to show for it.

So by small, we mean starting with one single recipe, one single source of juice, one single strain of yeast, and for your very first time making cider, you should only make one very small batch of just 1–5 gallons. That's it. No more. That brings us to the equipment you need and how to source it.

The Equipment

Fanning recommends starting with two 5-gallon *carboys*. A **carboy** isn't a kid who valets your car at the country club: it's a plastic or glass container that's used to ferment wine, cider, mead, or beer. It is sometimes called a *demijohn.* It looks like a giant wine jug or upside-down water cooler that you swiped from the office. They can be sold alone, or with a rubber stopper and a *fermentation lock*. A **fermentation lock,** also sometimes called an *airlock*, is basically a gadget that is designed to be filled with sanitized water, which keeps bacteria and other bad stuff out of the cider you're fermenting, but it also allows the carbon dioxide gas, produced by the yeasts, to escape without exploding. They're sometimes called bubblers. Some carboys can be purchased with this attachment. You will also need one rubber stopper or cork to cap it (also known as a *bung).*

Shabatura recommends going even smaller for your very first batch, making only one single gallon of cider so instead of a carboy, you'll need two glass gallon-sized jugs. If you purchased your cider in a jug, then you've got one of them, or you can reuse an old wine jug from your Aunt Edna's birthday party. For a one-gallon-jug, you need a drilled #6 size rubber stopper, and you will also need a fermentation lock.

You will also need plastic tubing to move the cider from one carboy or jug into the other one, and if you want to make your life a whole lot easier, Shabatura recommends using an *autosiphon*. An

A glass carboy, or jug for making cider.

autosiphon helps you move the cider from one container to another without any fuss. It's basically a pump that allows you to move the cider without overly agitating it or making a mess. Some autosiphons come with plastic tubing, but others do not.

Instead of using an autosiphon, you can use a racking cane, but both our experts say that they can be more difficult to use.

And you will need some food-grade plastic tubing. Shabatura recommends 3–6 feet of it. And the tubing needs to fit your equipment. For gallon jugs, use a $\frac{5}{16}$-inch size. If you're planning to make 5 gallons, you need to use a 6-gallon carboy. If you're planning to make 4 gallons, use a 5-gallon carboy. The rule is to have about 20 percent headspace.

You also will need an *oxidizer*. An **oxidizer** is a type of alkali cleaner you use *before* you sanitize your equipment. It, according to Shabatura, will get rid of the funk. You can do this with a solution like PBW (Powdered Brewery Wash), which Shabatura recommends, or you can use a mixture of bleach water (1 tablespoon of

You Can't Touch This—
or, Why Sanitation Matters

Your mom probably told you hundreds of times over the course of your childhood to wash your hands. We're going to tell you again—wash your hands! And then some.

If there's an itty-bitty, teeny-tiny, microscopic bit of bacteria on your hands before you touch your equipment and start making hard cider, chances are, you're gonna have bad cider.

And after you wash your hands thoroughly, then you need to clean the area you're going to make your cider in, and then you need to clean and sterilize your equipment.

Some people use a plastic bucket and lid as the place where they clean and sanitize their equipment. You can also bleach and/or sanitize a sink in which you then sanitize your equipment.

To clean or oxidize your equipment, you need to basically soak everything you're using in a bleach solution or an oxidizer like PBW. Scrub everything, then let it soak in the solution for at least 15 minutes and up to an hour. For bleach, you must let it sit for at least an hour. One mistake home cider makers make is to just spray things with a bleach solution, then immediately rinse it off—the bleach needs to time to do its job. Then, you have to rinse it off vigorously, so that no oxidizer or bleach should be left to flavor your cider. If you are using a stainless steel tank, bleach is not recommended because it can leave a residue.

Then you sterilize it with a food-grade sanitizer like Star San. Fanning and Shabatura recommend this brand because it doesn't leave any off-tastes in cider because it eventually breaks down into a simple sugar the yeast eats.

Soak all the equipment in the sanitizer. Make sure it's coated everything, then drain it, and let air dry, but don't rinse. If you're concerned, you can do as Shabatura advises, which is to swish in some bottled or just boiled water.

And clean and sanitize every single piece of equipment that will touch the cider, even peripherally, like measuring spoons or cups!

Cleaning and sterilizing isn't just important to make sure no one gets sick—just a small bit of contamination can ruin the taste of your cider. "Cleaning and sterilization is so important in making good cider," Shabatura says.

bleach per cup of water). You oxidize, then you sanitize, and check out the helpful sanitation sidebar.

You will also need a *sanitizer*. A **sanitizer** is what you need to sanitize your equipment and sterilize it so that it is free from germs. If you don't sanitize your equipment, very bad things can—and often, do—happen. One contaminated fingerprint on the inside of your jug or carboy can turn a whole batch into something undrinkable. The sanitizer both Fanning and Shabatura recommend for home cider makers is called Star San. You can also use iodine as a sanitizer. It must be noted, however, that iodine can stain everything a yellow-brown color, and you don't want to use straight iodine—you must mix it with water.

Any food-grade sanitizer does the job, however. Basically, you put a recommended amount of sanitizer into the exact specified amount of water, and then you sanitize your equipment after you've already cleaned and rinsed it. More on the importance of sanitation later.

Fanning also recommends getting a *hydrometer*. A **hydrometer** is a very scientific-looking (it looks like one of those cylinders you may have used in your high school chemistry class) yet very easy-to-use piece of equipment that will measure the alcohol content of your cider. Hydrometers measure the density of liquids. After yeast consumes the sugars in cider, making alcohol, the density drops. So, you measure the density at the start and through the process to determine when to rack and bottle your cider, Shabatura says.

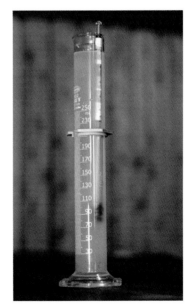

A hydrometer measures the density and determines the alcohol content of your cider.

You also need bottles or growlers, and if you use bottles, you will need bottle caps and perhaps a bottle capper or bottle filler. Basically, you just need something to store your finished product in.

If you want to test a little bit of your cider as you make it, get a *wine thief*. A **wine thief** is made out of glass or plastic, and basically, it takes little sneaky sips of cider out of a jug or carboy.

And, if you are like many people, you might want to add more fizz to your cider. In that case, you might want to use a soda stream or another method of adding extra carbonation. Shabatura swears by using the Fizz Giz Soda Rope (which she talks about at length on her website) for adding extra or "forced carbonation," at the end of the cider-making process.

"If I want to take a growler to a party, I run (the hard cider) through the Fizz Giz first," she says. "It's also great to make sparking water, and you can add carbonation to practically anything, including milk, but carbonated milk tastes awful."

If you want to control your yeast at the beginning and/or end of the fermentation process, you will use **Campden tablets**, or sodium metabisulfate, to prevent wild yeasts from growing at the beginning or your yeasts from starting to re-ferment after adding sugar (more on that in the Ingredients, Part Three). It doesn't stop an active fermentation. If you try to put a Campden tablet in the middle of the process, it will not stop the yeast from growing. But you can use it in the beginning before fermentation starts to prevent it, or you can use it at the end to prevent re-fermentation.

Most of this equipment can easily be purchased online, but you can also visit your local home brewing or winemaking supply store. Store personnel can also guide you on what you need for your type of home setup, and they also are great to call to troubleshoot any problems you might encounter.

You can also simply buy a home cider-making kit. Several home brewing and/or winemaking companies have assembled basic kits. They range in cost from about $40–$100, but Shabatura says the basics, if you buy them individually (and if you already have empty wine jugs or got some from a recycling center), should run you about $20–$30. You can also find used, or barely used, equipment on Craigslist and at rummage or garage sales, too.

Ingredients, Part One: The Juice

The two required ingredients for hard cider are apple juice and yeast, but within these two categories, oh, what a variety!

The juice is really where everything starts. And you can basically use any kind of apple juice whatsoever—pasteurized, unpasteurized, juice from a single type of apple, freshly pressed from the farm, from the juice aisle in your grocery store—basically anything that you like the taste of. Some cideries or orchards also sell their unfermented juice to home cider makers, and in some rare instances, you can even get juice blends from cider-making or heritage apples, but those are deliciously rare whereas regular farmhouse juice can be found at most apple orchards across the country and plenty of farmstand stores and even some grocery stores, especially in the fall, during harvest season.

You can use just about any type of apple juice (or, pear juice, if you're making perry), except for one, and this is a big exception: you *cannot* use juice that has preservatives in it, Shabatura says. Read the labels. Any preservatives whatsoever will kill the yeast, and your cider will not ferment. If you see an ingredient that you don't recognize—like potassium sulfate or sodium benzoate—don't buy it. It won't work. Period.

Shabatura says she used to see bottles of apple juice at the grocery store or Walmart all the time that contained preservatives, but they aren't as prevalent as they once were. But still, the first line of inquiry she poses to someone whose

cider-making experience was an epic fail is whether the juice they used contained preservatives. It's still common enough that people buy it, then try to make cider with it, and then fail miserably. So, read the labels.

Juice right from a farm usually will ferment into a more flavorful cider than some of the blander stuff you can find at your grocery store, but both will get the job done.

Shabatura cautions people about fermenting unpasteurized or raw cider because they can risk contamination, or in worse cases, illnesses, so her favorite cider to use is pasteurized cider from a farm. Some cider enthusiasts use Camden tablets if they're using unpasteurized juice, too (not just to control the yeast activity of their cider), but that isn't the same as pasteurization.

Fanning suggests people use what tastes the best to them.

What Shabatura really cautions against, even more than raw juice from a farm (because farmers, by law, cannot make juice from apples that have fallen on the ground and gotten contaminated by animal droppings or other stuff), is using the apples from your neighbor. Especially if any of them have dropped, even briefly, to the ground.

"You might not get E. coli from your kitchen, but you could get E. coli from your neighbor's dropped apples," Shabatura says, adding that her father's area of research was foodborne illnesses so she's really cognizant of that. "Getting sick doesn't need to be a part of your cider-making experience."

Ingredients, Part Two: The Yeast

While it seems obvious that the juice matters, the yeast does, too. Without the yeast, the juice would remain juice. The yeast not only converts the sugars in the juice into alcohol, but it also produces the carbon dioxide gas that will protect the cider from oxidizing during the fermentation process.

While raw juice has naturally found yeasts in it—and you could make cider without adding any additional yeasts to it, and that's how cider was initially made, for centuries—to control the process and the flavors, you need to use a good, commercial yeast, made especially for cider, beer, or wine.

Before we go into the different kinds of yeast out there that make good cider, we'll just state up front not to go buy the yeast from the baking aisle of your grocery store.

Bread yeasts and beverage fermenting yeasts are both yeasts, and, yes, there are dozens of websites touting how easy it is to make hard cider just using juice and bread yeast. But, well, yuck. Maybe the resulting ciders made from bread yeast will tempt your taste buds, but neither Fanning nor Shabatura recommend it.

The main reason to use a special yeast is that when you do—whether it's a yeast cultivated particularly for hard cider, for beer, or for wine—the yeast itself will impart flavors and aromas to the cider, as well as bring out flavors and aromas found naturally in the juice.

There are dozens of different fermentation yeasts on the market, and you can order them online, find them on home brewing and winemaking websites and stores, and even direct from the laboratories themselves. A lot of home cider makers are fond of champagne yeasts, but the main thing to look at when trying to decide between two different yeasts are the aromas that they produce. Find one that produces the aromas you're looking for.

Every yeast produces something a little bit different—or, a lot different. To demonstrate the different aromas that different yeasts produce, Fanning fermented three different, small batches: one using Wyeast cider yeast from Wyeast Laboratories, he used EC1118, a dry champagne yeast from Lalvin, and Fresco from Renaissance Yeast. He used the same juice blend from a culinary apple orchard, but the three resulting ciders boasted dramatically different aromas.

The 1118 cider boasted a crisp, dry apple aroma whereas the Renaissance offered bolder, more fruity characteristics, and the Wyeast presented milder aromas. They all produced a lovely cider, but they were quite different. "The yeast provides other characteristics that the juice alone won't provide," Fanning says.

And the one thing to note with different yeast strains is that different yeasts work better at different fermenting temperatures, Fanning points out. "All yeasts have a slightly different preference of where they want to be," Fanning says. "Most want to be in the range between 59 and 70, but they're all different."

One thing to note when selecting yeasts is that some yeasts produce less sulfur during the fermentation process than others. The Renaissance yeast is one such yeast, Fanning says. Ask the folks at your local home brew shop which yeasts have low sulfur or less of a low sulfur smell. "Some shops may or may not have these yeasts so you might have to order them online," Fanning says. "But always go to the local shop first to support your community. They also can help you while you're making your cider and answer questions, too."

Shabatura, who has fermented hard cider from dozens of different yeasts, says the four strains she uses are Nottingham Ale Yeast, Safcider 40725 Cider yeast, Lalvin E-1118, and Safale S-04 yeasts. Of those, her absolute favorite is Notthingham Ale Yeast. (For more information on why Shabatura LOVES these yeasts, check out her website, www.howtomakehardcider.com.)

But your palate might not be quite like hers or Fanning's, she points out. This is where you pick one yeast to start with—and then you take copious notes—and document what you did, what temperature you fermented at, etc. so that you know if the resulting product is to your taste. Experiment, but document, to figure out what works best for you.

This is also where purchasing your yeast from a local home-brewing or winemaking supply store can come in handy. It's very easy to get overwhelmed with the dozens and dozens of yeasts out there.

Ingredients, Part Three: The Extra Stuff

Fanning is a big believer in just using good juice and good yeast, but there are other ingredients you can add to your cider that can enhance or change its flavor profile—and we're not even talking about adding berries or herbs or hops!

You can add additional acids, like malic or a blend of malic, citric, and tartaric to balance out the acidity of your cider. If you do add acid, just add a little, teeny bit—start with ¼–½ teaspoon for a gallon of finished cider, and you can always add more.

If your cider is cloudy or hazy, you can filter it, using a filter, but you can also add a *pectic enzyme* like Pectinase. *Pectin*, which is the naturally occurring starch in apples that makes it fantastic for creating jellies, jams, and dried fruit leather, also naturally causes a cider to be cloudy. It doesn't affect the taste, but it does create an appearance that you might not like so you can use a **pectic enzyme**—add ½ teaspoon per gallon at the start of your cider making, to break down the pectin. Fanning says this isn't necessary, especially for someone who is making cider for the very first time at home. A cloudy cider doesn't taste necessarily any different from a clear cider, he points out.

Walker Fanning making cider in Madison, Wisconsin.

"If you're a home cider maker who is making cider for the first time, do you really care how crystal clear it is?" he says. "If you want it to be (clearer, but without using pectinase), the main thing is to not shake it up when you're moving it from one carboy to another so that all the sediment stays at the bottom of the bottle. If you want to do it later on, that's the next step."

If you are only making a gallon, you can do what is called cold crashing the cider. Place the gallon in a refrigerator for at least a day and up to a week. Under the cold conditions, the yeasts will clump together, and you can easily leave them behind when you rack cider.

Campden tablets or potassium metabisulfite are chemicals that produce sulfites, which then stop yeast from fermenting. They're generally used as a preservative and stabilizer. While they can be used before fermentation starts to stop wild yeasts from growing, they are most often after fermentation is completed to prevent re-fermentation after adding sugar (called backsweetening). They're like adding sulfites to wine, in a sense, and they often come in tablet form, and you use one tablet, crushed into a powder, per gallon of cider. To prevent re-fermentation before backsweetening you will need to use both campden tablets and **sorbate**, a potassium salt, to keep the yeasts from fermenting the new sugars.

Shabatura recommends using the Campden tablets if you're using raw or unpasteurized juice, but Fanning prefers letting those yeasts go forward in the making of the cider.

"If you halt those yeasts going forward, you're going to lose out on some delicate flavors," Fanning says.

Document Your Cider

Both Fanning and Shabatura are big fans of taking copious notes, photos, and other forms of documenting your cider as you make it, especially the very first time you do. "If you don't take really good notes, you won't be able to duplicate what you did," Fanning says.

Fanning recommends recording four things everyday: the date, the gravity, the temperature, and the tasting notes. He always removes samples every day to test the gravity and the taste, and he does so using an autosiphon to prevent contamination and to retain protective layer of carbon dioxide.

Otherwise, you also won't know what went wrong if something went wrong. Whether you document your cider making with your phone, on social media, or in a notebook, the main thing is to keep track of it as you make it. By taking good notes, you will also stay on top of your cider, and you will better understand how cider ferments in your home or apartment (or cottage or garage), and you'll know if fermenting it in one area of the basement is better than another.

Fanning does advise home cider makers who want to use sugar, honey, or maple syrup as a backsweetener that Campden tablets and sorbate are the easiest way to prevent re-fermentation before you add the sugar. Other methods, include home pasteurization, can be more difficult and perhaps even a bit dangerous, as they involve boiling the cider in containers on the stove.

Speaking of backsweetening, you can also add brown sugar, honey, dextrose, white sugar, stevia, and even natural apple flavorings, which you can either find at the grocery store or order online. Shabatura likes using sugars like stevia or Splenda that yeasts don't break down if you use them to add extra sweetness.

Other ingredients for home cider making include yeast nutrients (products that help feed the yeast), extra tannins, acids, and practically any additional fruit or spice, too, for flavoring. **Malic acid**, the natural acid found in apples, can be added if a cider is especially weak or watery tasting.

Walker Fanning's Basic Cider Instructions for Home Cider Enthusiasts

This is a dry, lovely cider recipe without any extra additives. But the notes below offer some suggested variations.

1–5 gallons apple juice, no preservatives added
1 packet (about 5 grams) of yeast
Cane sugar, if needed
Campden tablets (1 per gallon)
Sorbate (¾ tsp. per gallon)
Honey to taste (2¼ tsp. per gallon for a semisweet cider)

After having cleaned and sterilized all of the equipment (and we mean ALL of the equipment, including that plastic funnel you're using to pour the juice into your jug or carboy), measure the sugar level of your juice in the hydrometer. It should be from 1.035–1.050 S.G. Under that 1.035, add sugar to get to that 5 percent benchmark.

Note: The measurement of 1.050 is pretty typical for most apple juices. To increase the gravity by 0.005, add 1.7 oz. per gallon of cider.

Then, pour the juice into a jug or carboy. Add the yeast, then attach the lid or stopper (with a hole for the airlock) and attach the airlock on top.

Place your jug or carboy out of direct sunlight in a room with a temperature of anywhere in the range 55–70 degrees, with 59 degrees Fahrenheit being the optimal temperature. The main thing, Fanning says, is that you don't want the temperature to go above 80 degrees, as the cider will ferment really fast and could develop a powdery taste.

"Basements work really, really well since they are often in the 60s down there," Fanning says. But don't ferment your cider in your basement if it is musky. "That flavor will come through in your finished cider," he cautions.

If you want to prevent wild yeast, you add your Campden tablet at rate of 1 tablet per gallon, then wait twenty-four hours before adding the yeast.

Fermentation will start as soon as you add yeast, and it will continue for 8–12 days. This is the active fermentation stage. Check your fermentation everyday, and take notes. The cider will start buvbbling, then develop a frothy head, and as it ferments, it will get bigger, then get smaller until there's almost nothing bubbling.

Walker Fanning shows off three different cider varieties he makes.

This means that the fermentation has slowed down or stopped. You will then use your autosiphon to move the cider to your second sanitized jug or carboy, leaving the sediment on the bottom behind.

Pour a little sample out, or remove a sample with a wine thief to test its sugar levels with the hydrometer (you can also taste it to see its progress).

At this point, fermentation is done, so you want to transfer the cider into a new, clean and sanitized jug or carboy. Then, add the Campden tablets at a rate of 1 tablet per gallon and ¾ teaspoon sorbate per gallon, and reattach the airlock. After three days, taste the cider, then add the honey to get it to the level of sweetness you so desire. To properly backsweeten a cider, you will need to heat up the honey (with some water or cider) to only about 120 degrees—enough for it to dissolve, then add it to the cider.

Insipid or Watery Cider, Now What?

So, you've taken copious notes, done your homework, and to the best of your knowledge, you've done everything right, so how come your cider tastes watery? The main thing that could have happened, depending on the apple blend that went into the juice, is that it's not acidic enough. "If you got your juice from an orchard, hopefully the orchard used a mix of sweet and tart apples, but sometimes you will get a mix that's not really very tart at all," Fanning says.

"To correct that, you add malic acid in ¼ teaspoon per gallon increments, and then you mix it really well," Fanning says. Then you taste it after the first addition of acid, and if you need to add a little more acid, you can add more. The important thing is to mix it really well so that it's completely dissolved and distributed throughout the cider. Be careful not to add too much—an excess of malic acid can cause heartburn.

Some orchards, Fanning notes, might use as many as 15–20 different kinds of apples in their juice. "Then it tastes like a symphony," he says.

But do taste it as it ages to see if it is to your liking. When you think it's ready for bottling, use the hydrometer to check its final gravity. You will want a final gravity of 1.005–0.9976 S.G. Bottle the cider, and after two weeks, enjoy.

Then let it sit for an additional 2–3 weeks, checking and tasting frequently to see how it develops, then rack and bottle the cider. You can even let it rest longer—some do for 2–4 months, but for first-time cider makers, Fanning recommends only 2–3 weeks. The important thing is to taste it, then bottle it when it's to your liking.

"You can, however, bottle it without waiting 2–3 weeks, but if you bottle it right away, it will taste really yeasty," Fanning says.

Variations

Once you've mastered one cider and got its sugar levels to your liking, you can always add herbs, other juices, or other components. Shabatura recommends adding natural flavor extracts (she prefers OliveNation brand) to add cinnamon or raspberry or apple, to give your cider a bit more *oomph*. But other people recommend using the actual spices or fruits. Start with about 1–4 cups of fruit per gallon of cider, and take notes to see where your taste preferences land. With spices, hops, and other ingredients, start with a ¼ cup (and that's whole spices, not ground cinnamon, for example). Add them, perhaps in a cloth tea bag, to your gallon or carboy.

Fanning loves using real spices and herbs. He suggests adding them right after fermentation has stopped. If you want a cinnamon cider, Fanning recommends just shaving a little bit of cinnamon directly from a cinnamon stick into your carboy after fermentation. But test a little bit of it first in a smaller container, to see exactly how much you want to flavor your cider.

The Cider Rules,
According to Jessica Shabatura

Jessica Shabatura knows what works and doesn't work when it comes to making hard cider at home. And after answering hundreds and hundreds of emails from people whose cider-making attempts have failed, she's got a list of eight rules that you must follow if you don't want to have an epic fail. If you've just skimmed through this chapter and are diving right into making some homemade hard cider, read and follow these rules first!

Here are her rules for making homemade cider:

1. Sterilize your equipment. And your hands. If you don't completely sterilize everything your cider will come in contact with, you could end up with a nasty batch. As she puts it on her blog: trouble is expensive, and it tastes like vinegar.
2. Unless you have your own orchard, buy your juice from a store (or orchard). "If you don't clean your equipment perfectly, you won't come down with food poisoning, but if you get juice from your neighbor, you could get e. coli from your neighbor's dropped apples," she says.
3. Make sure the juice doesn't have any preservatives in it. At all. When people contact her through her website after their first batch of cider failed, that's the first question she asks. If your nonalcoholic apple cider has anything listed in its ingredients that you can't pronounce, don't buy it. Preservatives prevent yeast from working.
4. Start small. It's easy to get really, really, really excited, and you decide you're going to make 15 gallons of hard cider . . . and then you fail and never make hard cider ever again. Start with one to five gallons, max. Smaller amounts yield to better control, and better control leads to better outcomes.
5. Experiment with yeasts, sugars, and other cider-making variables to find what tastes best to your palate. "If you're going to go with five gallons, don't just dump everything into one big bucket, because if you make a mistake, you've wasted a lot of time and money on something that sucks," Shabatura says. "This is the voice of experience speaking. Once, I got really excited and decided to make spiced cider, and I dumped a bunch of cinnamon sticks into an entire batch. It literally tasted like gym socks—it was so horrible."

6. Take copious notes of what you do with each batch of cider. That way, if it tastes amazing, you can make it again. "You now have my permission to make five gallons of that," she says. If you don't take notes of the exact types of yeast, sugar, additives, temperatures, etc., then you won't be able to make that cider again.

7. And even if you do make that cider again, exactly, it might taste a little different. "It makes a difference at what time of the day the apples were picked or if there was a dry spell . . . there are all these different variables," she says. Which is what makes cider making exciting. And it's what also makes it important to control everything that's within your control—i.e. equipment, cleanliness, exact measurements in recipes.

8. Make sure you're passionate about making it. Craigslist is filled with advertisements of barely used cider, beer, and wine-making equipment. "And they often have the phrase 'because my spouse is making me get rid of this' attached to their ads," she quips. Before you invest a lot of money and time into a hobby you're not sure you want to enter into, make sure you're passionate about it. A good rule of thumb is: if you make your own bread, you'd probably have fun making your own cider. If you think that is why grocery stores were invented, then maybe you just want to go to the liquor store to buy your hard cider instead of making it yourself.

CHAPTER 7

Sip It, Shake It, Stir It: Cider Cocktail Recipes and Variations, plus Cider Cocktail Guidelines and More

"I know how the nuts taken in conjunction with winter
apples, cider, and doughnuts, make old people's tales and
old jokes sound fresh and crisp and enchanting."
—Mark Twain

CIDER IS NOT JUST A spectacular beverage all by itself, but it also can be a great ingredient in cocktails. Cider was an ingredient in one of the very first cocktails ever invented, called the Stone Fence, which was what soldiers in the American Revolution drank to stay fortified between battles. But besides the revival of this too-old-to-even-be-considered-classic cocktail, bartenders are using it in inventive drinks that range the spectrum.

Cider can be substituted in many different cocktail recipes, but the two primary ways are either to lower the alcohol content or increase the alcohol content of the drink, points out Mattie Beason, owner of Black Twig Cider House, in Durham, North Carolina, which boasts the largest collection of cider in the Southeast and the only indoor *txotx* (pronounced CHO-ch, Basque country cider barrel, which aerates still cider as it is shot out from the barrel into the glass) in the country.

In the case of lower proof drinks, cider can replace any white alcohol in an array of different cocktails. That means it can replace vodka, gin, rum, and tequila with ease. A cider daiquiri, especially if made with a refreshing lime hard cider, can be a delightful alternative to Hemingway's classic cocktail. It's lovely as a substitute for gin in a negroni, and it plays quite well with cranberry juice, especially if it is cran-apple, in a cosmo.

It also can easily substitute for tonic water, seltzer, or any kind of soda in a cocktail, giving an extra kick to any fizzy drink. "When you substitute cider for club soda, it adds flavor and more aromatics to the cocktail," Beason says.

That said, cider also tends to play quite well with bourbon and many different kinds of whiskey, and it can also be easily substituted for for beer, wine, and champagne in cocktails.

But one thing to note—and it should seem obvious—is to really understand the flavor of the cider you're planning to use in a cocktail, says Ambrosia Borowski, assistant general manager of the Northman cider bar and restaurant in Chicago.

"One of the tricky things you have to watch out for is some ciders have high tannins, and some have a surprising amount of acid," she says. "If you're using an American cider, and you want to add it to a liquor like rye, and if you add a cider that has either a lot of tannins or high acid, that is going to lash out in the cocktail because rye is already astringent and bitter so the drink will become extreme and unpleasant."

In that case, she says, "You'd be better off going with a low acid cider like an English pub cider or a sweeter American cider."

Taste, taste, taste the cider before you add it to your cocktail. Is it sweet or dry? Is it complex or single noted? Is there a flavor component to the cider—like strawberry or hops? Most great cocktails have a balance of sweet, bitter, and/or sour, so if you understand the flavor and the components of the cider you're thinking of adding to a cocktail, you'll have a better idea what the resulting cocktail will taste like before you make it.

Also, unless the cider is still, it's best to stir, instead of shake, the cocktail. If the cocktail needs shaking—which if it has cream or egg whites in it, it will—shake the ingredients before adding the effervescent cider into it. Or, gently transfer it from one glass to another in place of shaking.

Spirited Apple Beverages to Add to Your Cocktail

Cider has been distilled into some delicious apple spirits for centuries. Perhaps the most famous is *calvados* or French apple brandy. There's also American apple brandy, sometimes known as applejack, but as discussed in chapter 1, applejack also can mean a blend of apple brandy with a neutral spirit like whiskey.

Besides Laird's, which has been making applejack since before the United States was a country, other brandy makers are making some high-quality apple brandies, including Copper & Kings (whose founder actu-

Eleanor Leger makes not only ciders from apples she grows, but also Orleans, cider-based aperitifs, at Eden Specialty Ciders in Vermont.

ally started the Crispin hard cider brand before he sold it to MillerCoors).

Applejack is used in the traditional Jack Rose cocktail (featured later in this chapter), and both regular apple brandy and calvados can be used in any cocktail that calls for brandy or substituted for whiskey in cocktails.

Cider-based aperitifs are another liquor to add to your cider cocktails. Eden Specialty Ciders in Vermont makes a line of three of these liqueurs flavored with herbs, spices, and roots called Orleans, including Bitter, Wood, and Herbal. Any of the Orleans lineup can be substituted in cocktails that call for Aperol, Campari, or other European

aperitivos, but they're not exact counterparts to European versions, as they're made only with local ingredients found in Vermont. A simple way to enjoy any of the Orleans lineups with hard cider is to just pour 1½–2 ounces of Orleans in a glass and top with hard cider.

Orleans Bitter goes extremely well in a negroni with a good vermouth and a good gin while Wood can add a lovely note to Manhattans, and Herbal plays quite well with gin, too. "We make 22 different products, and this is my favorite," says Eleanor Leger, founder of Eden Specialty Ciders.

Ice ciders and pommeau can also be added to cocktails. But because they are so refined and sweet, use them as you would a fine liqueur—just a little bit added to a sparkling cider cocktail can be quite exquisite.

Equipping Your Bar

The absolute basics you need to outfit your home bar are: a shaker, a jigger, a bar spoon, and glasses. If you don't have a cobbler shaker—the kind with a built-in strainer—you will also need a strainer. Most professional bars also have Hawthorne strainers (the kind with a spring attached that fits over the top of the shaker), and they often have julep and/or tea strainers. A home bar doesn't absolutely need all of these different strainers, but they're nice to have for the rare occasions you need them. The main thing is to get a good shaker that fits your hand and that you enjoy using.

As far as jiggers go, all jiggers aren't created equal. We don't know about you, but unless you're making dozens of drinks a night (and if you're not a professional, you likely are not!), you probably can't eyeball a quarter of an ounce inside an unmarked jigger. So do yourself a favor and buy yourself a jigger that has little concentric circles inside it indicating what measures ¼, ½, ¾, 1, 1½, and 2 ounces.

Oxo and Cocktail Kingdom are two brands that make such jiggers, and actually, professional bar instructors (who get paid good money to teach other professional bartenders) prefer these jiggers because exact measurements make better drinks. Cocktail making is more akin to baking than cooking—exact measuring can make your drinks taste a lot better!

If you don't have a bar spoon, you can swipe a larger spoon from your kitchen, but it won't work quite as easily for stirring drinks. If you like drinks with fruit and/or herbs, you might want to get a muddler. You can muddle ingredients with spoons, but muddlers work much better, and they're not expensive.

As far as cocktail glasses go, there are more than a dozen different kinds of glasses you can choose from, but you don't have to buy every glass on the market. If you had to just pick two (specifically made for cocktails), get a few martini or coupe (old-fashioned champagne glasses) for straight-up drinks, and pick a style of rocks or highball glasses for those on the rocks or blended. Or just use mason jars. Whatever glasses you enjoy drinking from are the glasses you should have behind your home bar.

But one thing to note with glasses is that size does matter. A 4-ounce drink looks pretty darn dinky in an 8-oz. glass, but it fits perfectly in a 6-ounce glass. And if you have really large glasses, you will need to double a recipe to fill those glasses . . . and then, you need to note you're drinking two-for-one.

In the recipes that follow, different glasses are listed for some of the cocktails, but you can drink them in whatever glass you prefer.

Ingredients

Just as life is too short to drink bad cider, it's also too short to drink bad booze. Buy the best quality you can afford, but also, buy what you like. While some recipes have very specific ingredients, you can easily substitute one type of bourbon for another or one type of bitters for another. The resulting drink might not taste quite the same as its creator intended, but it will probably still taste quite good.

Freshly squeezed juices taste oh-so-much better, and while you can use Rose's Lime Juice instead of fresh lime juice, the added sugar and preservatives will not improve the taste of your drink. If you don't like squeezing your own, Industry Juice (industryjuice .com) makes freshly squeezed juices for bars, and you can order its products online.

Basic Recipes to Enhance Cocktails: Simple Syrups, Grenadine, and Shrubs

Though the cocktail recipes in this chapter are meant to be as accessible to both home enthusiasts and professionals, if you're not particularly knowledgeable about cocktails, then this short section is for you. Simple syrups and shrubs are some of the common ingredients in cocktails, and they work extremely well with cider cocktails.

A **simple syrup** is simply sugar water, equal parts sugar and water. Some bartenders prefer using a greater ratio of sugar to water, but start with equal parts, and if you prefer things sweeter, just add a little more.

For starters, just dissolve ½ cup sugar into ½ cup warm water—you can heat it up in a pan or the microwave, or just take it straight from the hot water spigot.

Simple syrups can become a little more complex if you use a different sugar—try turbinado or another sugar in the raw (with some molasses left behind) to add some complexity. Straight brown sugar, especially when combined with cinnamon or nutmeg, can be a different addition to a cocktail. And using honey or maple syrup also changes the recipe.

Simple syrups can also become flavor enhancers when you add fresh herbs or spices, and a little bit can add a lot of flavoring. Lavender and hibiscus flowers can be added, so can different teas. They all can add a different dimension to your cocktails.

Basic Simple Syrup Recipe

This recipe is simple, but it can be used in many, many different cocktail recipes.

½ cup sugar
½ cup hot water

Whisk the ingredients together until sugar is completely dissolved.

Variations: For honey syrup, replace sugar with equal amount of honey. For maple syrup, replace sugar with an equal amount of maple syrup. For agave, replace sugar with equal amount of agave syrup.

Mint Syrup Recipe

Joy Perrine, the bad girl of bourbon, a legendary bartender in Kentucky, taught us how to make the perfect mint syrup, and this is it. Not only is it good for mint juleps, but it's also fantastic in mojitos, margaritas, gin and tonics, etc.

2 cups water
2 cups sugar
1 very large bunch fresh mint leaves, about 20 to 30 leaves

Heat all ingredients, stirring frequently until boiling, over medium-high heat on the stove. As soon as it boils, turn off the stove, and remove from heat. Cover, and let sit at room temperature for up to twenty-four hours. Strain, and use.

Variations: You can make a different herbal simple syrup by replacing the mint with sage, thyme, rosemary, basil. You name it, you can use it in a syrup. The only thing is, they should be fresh, otherwise they won't quite flavor the syrup the same way.

Cinnamon Simple Syrup

Cinnamon goes so well with apples, so this cinnamon simple syrup is fantastic in cider cocktails.

1 cup brown sugar
1 cup water
5–7 cinnamon sticks

Bring everything to a boil over medium high heat, stirring frequently. Once boiling, remove from heat, then let sit, covered, for 2 hours.

Lavender Simple Syrup

Lavender pairs really nicely with gin-based cocktails.

1 cup sugar
1 cup water
1 tbsp. dried lavender blossoms

Bring everything to a boil, stirring frequently. Let completely cool, strain out the lavender, and use.

Homemade Grenadine

A lot of recipes call for grenadine, but traditionally, grenadine was a pomegranate sugar syrup, not the artificially colored and flavored thing we think of today. It's also a traditional ingredient in a Jack Rose cocktail.

2 cups fresh pomegranate juice
2 cups sugar
⅛ tsp. rosewater

Bring pomegranate juice to a boil over medium-high heat. Reduce heat to medium-low, stir in the sugar until it is completely dissolved, then remove from heat and let cool to room temperature. Stir in the rosewater and use.

Shrubs are basically equal parts vinegar, sugar, and fresh fruit, let to sit at room temperature covered for about twenty-four hours. If you use a different sugar, you get a different shrub. If you use a different vinegar, you get a different shrub. If you use a different fruit, you get a different shrub. Try a balsamic vinegar with strawberries and brown sugar, apples with apple cider vinegar and regular cane sugar, or try a red wine vinegar with raspberries and maple syrup. It's all up to you.

Shrubs are actually drinks with a long history that were once used not just to flavor cocktails, but were also enjoyed straight up on hot days.

Basic Apple Shrub

Apples, of course, go very well with cider-based recipes.

1 cup grated apple (with peel, but not core or seeds)
1 cup sugar
1 cup apple cider vinegar

Place all ingredients in a glass or plastic bowl, cover with plastic wrap, and let sit at room temperature for twenty-four hours. Strain out the apples using a fine mesh strainer and pressing on the bits of apple to get all the remaining liquid. Enjoy in cocktails, or with about equal parts seltzer water.

Basic Berry Shrub

1 cup raspberries
1 cup sugar
1 cup raspberry vinegar, apple cider vinegar, or white balsamic vinegar

Place all ingredients in a glass or plastic bowl, cover with plastic wrap, and let sit at room temperature for twenty-four hours. Strain out the berries using a fine mesh strainer and pressing on the bits of fruit to get all the remaining liquid. Enjoy in cocktails, or with about equal parts seltzer water.

Now that you have recipes for simple syrups and shrubs, you can get into the heart of this chapter—making *cocktails*!

Cocktails are basically drinks that have a balance of sweet, sour, bitter, and booze. Some cocktails are more booze-forward while some cocktails emphasize the sweet notes. In general, though, cocktails have a balance of flavors, and even a booze-forward cocktail shouldn't make you grimace because it's too boozy.

That said, what you think is balanced is not necessarily what someone else thinks is balanced, so our advice is to please your own taste buds. If you think a cocktail needs bit more sweetness, then add a little more simple syrup. If it's not sour enough, add a little more juice. And if it's too weak, then add just a little bit more booze.

But our rule of thumb for adding more of anything is to add only ¼ ounce more of something at a time. For example, add ¼ ounce more simple syrup, stir or shake it, then taste. You can always add more if it's not to your liking, but you can't dial it back after you've already added it.

The Stone Fence

As perhaps the very first cider cocktail in history, this drink was first served in taverns around the time of the American Revolution, and it became a popular drink in the early 1800s. It's basically a shot mixed in with a draft of cider, and it was made with whatever local spirits and local ciders were available.

12–14 oz. cider
2 oz. spirit of choice

Gently stir spirit with bar spoon in a cocktail shaker filled with ice. Pour cider into a pint glass, strain chilled spirit into cider, gently stir, and enjoy.

Variations, Part 1: Pair a barrel-aged gin with a hopped cider, a dark rum with a sweet cider, bourbon with a barrel-aged cider, or a rosé cider with a fruity liqueur or fruit-infused vodka.

Variations, Part 2: Add a dash of Angostura or Peychaud's bitters and/or a squeeze of lemon juice (about ¼ an ounce).

Spice Is Nice

This is another lovely recipe from Ramborn. Whiskey or bourbon blends with cider, Worcestershire sauce, black pepper, and cardamom pods.

2 oz. whiskey
2 grinds of fresh black pepper
1–2 tsp. gently crushed cardamom pods
1 drop Worcestershire sauce
4–6 oz. Ramborn medium dry cider

Stir all ingredients together in a rocks glass filled with ice.

Mulled Cider or Wassail

As long as people have been drinking hard cider in cold climates, they've been warming up to mulled cider. And this tastes good on a cold winter's night.

2 quarts hard cider

2 sticks cinnamon

6 whole cloves

2 whole cardamom pods

1 vanilla bean, scraped

1-inch fresh ginger, peeled

Zest of 1 orange

Zest of 1 lemon

Pour all ingredients into a pot over low heat. Heat everything until completely warmed through, but not boiling. While wassail is warming, bring a separate pot or teapot of water to boil. Pour water into cups to heat them, then discard. Pour wassail into warmed cups, garnish with a peel of lemon or orange and a cinnamon stick.

Boozier Variation: Add 2 ounces of applejack, whiskey, bourbon, rum, or whiskey to each cup. And here's a trick from professional bartenders to keep the drinks from going lukewarm: Warm a large pot of water to simmering. Remove from heat, then stick the bottle of booze into the pot of water to warm the booze before adding to the cocktail.

Colonial Cider Flip

Made with beer or cider, this is a colonial drink that varied from tavern to tavern. Basically, eggs and sugar or molasses were frothed up, then warm beer or cider was added, and then the two were poured from one glass to another until sufficiently frothed and warm. It's easier to make using a microwave and a blender.

2 eggs
1–2 tbsp. sugar
2 oz. applejack or rum
12 oz. cider
1 dash Angostura bitters

In a high-speed blender, blend eggs, sugar, and spirit for 30 seconds. Meanwhile, pour the cider in a very large glass or bowl, place it in the microwave, and microwave on high for 45 seconds. Then, using two very large glasses or pitchers, pour the egg mixture into the warmed cider (if they are not large enough, they will froth over). Then, pour into a large pint glass for a single serving or divide among two medium-sized chalice-shaped beer glasses, then top with a dash of Angostura bitters.

Black Velvet

Cider can be substituted for beer in cocktails, but it also can be combined with beer for this very refreshing cocktail. For contrasting flavors, use a sweet or light cider; for more similar flavors, use a coffee-infused stout-like cider.

8 oz. cider
8 oz. stout beer

Pour cider into a pint glass, then pour in stout, and stir. Or, pour in cider, then gently pour the stout over an upside-down bar spoon, just above the cider to float the stout on top.

Cider Radler

A radler is basically grapefruit juice or soda combined with beer. Cider adds a more refreshing, fruity take on this summer drink.

8 oz. cider
8 oz. grapefruit soda or juice
Garnish of grapefruit peel

Gently stir all ingredients together in a pint glass. Garnish with a grapefruit peel.

Notes and Variations: TopNote Tonics and Q Tonics both make delicious, not-too-sweet grapefruit sodas. For a variation, add 1½ oz. Paula's Grapefruit Liqueur to give it a boozy twist.

Cider Mule

Cider plays well with ginger beer and lime juice, too.

8 oz. cider (possibly a ginger cider to enhance the ginger in the cocktail)
8 oz. ginger beer
¾ oz. freshly squeezed lime juice
Slice or wheel of lime, for garnish

Stir ingredients together gently into a pint glass. Garnish with lime.

Variations: To make this more like a Moscow mule, add 1½ oz. vodka to the mix. Instead of lime juice, substitute an apple shrub (page 136).

Cider Shandy

Beer and lemonade make for fast summer friends, but cider goes even better.

8 oz. cider
8 oz. lemonade (recipe below)
Lemon wheel, for garnish

Stir cider and lemonade together gently in a pint glass. Garnish with a lemon wheel. Tastes especially good with homemade lemonade.

Variation: Add ¾ oz. berry shrub (page 136) for a berry blast, and use a berry or rosé cider.

Homemade Lemonade

4 cups water
4 lemons, juiced
1 cup sugar

Combine all ingredients until sugar is dissolved.

Snakebite

Cider. Beer. Together. Enough said.

8 oz. English cider
8 oz. English lager

Stir both ingredients together gently in a pint glass.

Variation: add 1 tsp. cassis liqueur into the glass to give it an extra kick.

Kir *Cidre*

A kir is simply white wine with crème de cassis blackberry liqueur.

¾ oz. crème de cassis
4 oz. dry, still cider or sparkling cider
Blackberry, for garnish

Pour liqueur into bottom of a champagne flute. Top with cider. Garnish with a blackberry.

Kir *Cidre* Royal

A kir royale simply subs out the still wine for sparkling wine.

¾ oz. crème de cassis
4 oz. dry, sparkling French-style cider
Blackberry, for garnish

Pour liqueur into bottom of a champagne flute. Top with cider. Garnish with a blackberry.

Variation: Instead of crème de cassis, use Chambord raspberry liqueur, and garnish with a fresh raspberry instead of blackberry. Or, use an iced cider or pommeau instead of the crème de cassis.

Cider and Shrub

This is just a simple yet fun and refreshing recipe. You can use any type of cider and any type of shrub in this recipe—match them (a berry cider and a berry shrub) or mix them up (a berry shrub and a hoppy cider).

2 oz. shrub
4 to 6 oz. cider

Stir ingredients together gently, and serve in a coup or champagne flute.

Cider Mimosa

Nothing says brunch like a mimosa, and mimosas taste wonderful with a dry heritage cider.

2 oz. freshly squeezed orange juice
4 oz. dry heritage cider

Pour orange juice in a glass, top with cider, stir gently, and serve.

Cider Bellini

This fizzy cocktail also works well at brunch.

2 oz. peach puree
4 oz. dry heritage cider
Peach slice, for garnish

Pour peach puree into glass, top with cider, stir gently, and serve. Garnish with peach slice.

Variation: Instead of using peach puree, make a peach and white balsamic shrub instead.

Cider Champagne Cocktail

This fizzy, celebratory cocktail is simply delicious.

1 sugar cube
3–5 dashes Angostura bitters
4 oz. dry, sparkling heritage cider

Put sugar cube onto bottom of champagne flute. Top with 3–5 dashes of bitters. Pour cider on top.

Cider Sangria

Cider is the ultimate party punch in the summer, and while it can be made with red, white, or rosé wines, it can also be made with cider, especially if apple brandy is used instead of regular brandy. Any kind of cider works well with this cocktail, but try fruit ciders, rosé ciders, and herbed ciders for fun flavors.

1 apple, cored and sliced, then topped with juice from 1 lemon (to prevent browning)
1 lemon, sliced
1 orange, sliced
3 tbsp. sugar
6 dashes orange bitters
½ cup rum
½ cup orange liqueur
½ cup apple brandy
1 750 ml. bottle of cider
1–2 cups ice

In the bottom of a pitcher, stir together fruit, sugar, and bitters. Top with rum, orange liqueur, and brandy, and stir again. Let sit for 20–30 minutes in the refrigerator. Add cider, and stir again. Add ice. Serve immediately, or chill until ready to entertain. To serve, pour into glasses filled with ice, and additional fruit slices if desired. Makes about 6–8 servings.

Quick and Simple Cider Sangria Simplified

Sometimes you just want a glass of sangria, and you want it quick. But the different liquors take time to meld with the fruit and cider. If you don't have time, instead use Drambuie, a honey-based, Scotch liqueur that has a lot of complexity.

1½ oz. Drambuie
4–6 oz. cider
Apple slices and/or citrus slices

Stir all ingredients together with ice, and enjoy.

Sidra Sangria with Berries
From Virtue Cider

1 cup fresh berries
1 cup oranges, lemons, and limes, sliced
½ oz. rose water
1 cup pink grapefruit juice
2 oz. apple brandy
24 oz. Virtue Cider
Ice

Combine fruit, rose water, grapefruit juice, and brandy. Let sit for at least 10 minutes. Just before serving, add cider, and serve in tall glasses over ice.

Cider Sangria
by Lars Koch of Old Sugar Distillery, Madison, Wisconsin
This is another twist on sangria, using a grape liqueur and cherry juice—it's refreshing and quick to make.

4 cherries
½ oz. cherry juice
1 oz. Mitchell's Concord Grape Liqueur
4 oz. Hidden Cave Hibiscus Juniper Cider
Ice
Grapefruit Peel

Muddle four cherries in cherry juice, then add grape liqueur, cider, and a bit of ice. Stir everything together gently in a tall glass. Then twist a grapefruit peel 6 inches above the cocktail to spritz with oils, and drop in the cocktail for garnish.

The Grobe
by Dave Van, of Old Sugar Distillery, Madison, Wisconsin
This citrus cocktail isn't too sweet, but it's highly refreshing.

3 oz. Hidden Cave Rose Hip Rosemary cider
1 oz. grapefruit juice
½ oz. maple syrup
½ oz. apple brandy

Stir all ingredients together lightly with ice, and strain into a short glass.

The Argus

by Dave Van of Old Sugar Distillery, Madison, Wisconsin

This cocktail boasts honey, lemon, and lavender notes.

2 oz. Hidden Cave Lavender Lemongrass cider

1 oz. honey liquor

1 oz. fresh lemon juice

Splash of cherry juice

1 dash Angostura bitters

Stir all ingredients together with ice in a glass.

Summer Music

by Joe Matura of Old Sugar Distillery, Madison, Wisconsin

*This cocktail is not only refreshing—like a lavender-flavored lemonade—
but it's a cocktail with a low alcohol content, which makes it perfect for
indulging.*

4 oz. Hidden Cave Lavender Lemongrass cider

½ oz. maple syrup

¼ lemon

Pour cider and maple syrup into a tall glass, stir gently to combine.
Top with ice, then squeeze the lemon over. Discard the lemon and
serve.

The Sean Penn
By Mattie Beason, owner of The Black Twig Cider House in Durham, North Carolina

Beason, loves working with the individual nuances of different ciders to play up those characteristics in cocktails. The Sean Penn is basically a margarita enhanced by a shot of spicy cider, which adds a bit of heat and brings out the fruitiness of both the lime juice and the orange liqueur. "It's basically a margarita with a spicy cider by Blake's Hard Cider in Michigan called El Chavo," says Beason. "The cider gives the cocktail more spice and a fruitiness. The cider is interesting by itself, but with the cocktail, it becomes even more interesting."

1½ oz. Don Julio Blanco (or some Blanco tequila)
¾ oz. Cointreau (or another orange liqueur)
¾ oz. freshly squeezed lime juice
1¼ oz. Blake's El Chavo (or another spicy cider)
Lime wedge
Salt

Pour tequila, Cointreau, and lime juice into a shaker filled with ice. Shake for 60 seconds or until well chilled. Prepare rocks glass by rubbing with a lime wedge, then dipping in salt. Add ice to rocks glass, pour in spirits, then float cider on top, and add a lime wedge.

The Transcendent Crab
by Ambrosia Borowski

Borowski, who is the assistant manager of the Northman cider bar in Chicago, is one of the most knowledgeable cider folks in the bar business, and she knows her way around both cider and booze. Her cocktails are nothing short of sublime.

1 oz. Averna
¾ oz. Cynar 70
7 dashes Peychaud's Bitters
Anthem Hops cider
Smashed mint leaf

Stir together Averna, Cynar, and bitters, then strain into an 8-oz. glass filled with fresh ice.

Top with Anthem Hops (or any other hopped cider) and stir to incorporate.

Garnish with a smashed mint leaf.

Lavender Sparkler

Lavender and apple go together quite well. Gin and lavender go together quite well. Combine all three, and you've got a sparkling cocktail. For extra lavender emphasis, try a lavender cider.

1½ oz. gin, preferably an aromatic gin with some citrus (Hendrick's, North Shore No. 6, Rehorst, and Nolet's all work well)
¾ oz. lavender simple syrup
¾ oz. lemon juice
3 to 4 oz. cider
Fresh lavender and lemon slice, for garnish

In a shaker filled with ice, shake gin, lavender simple syrup, and lemon juice for 30–60 seconds. Strain into a Collins or rocks glass, top with cider, stir gently, then add garnish.

Rosé Cider Spritz

Spritz are typically made by combining wine with seltzer or bubbly wine with a low proof and often bitter alcohol. Rosé cider subs in nicely for the wine, and instead of Aperol, you can use the cider-based Orleans liqueur.

4 oz. rosé cider
1 oz. Aperol or Orleans Bitter liqueur
Lemon peel and strawberry, for garnish

Pour all ingredients into a champagne glass or coup. Stir gently, add garnish, and enjoy.

Apple Sidecar

A sidecar is a classic cocktail that is always made with brandy, lemon juice, and orange liqueur. It tastes fantastic when apple brandy is used.

1½ oz. apple brandy or calvados
¾ oz. orange liqueur
¾ oz. fresh lemon juice Lemon peel and apple slice, for garnish

Shake all ingredients together with ice in a shaker for 30–60 seconds. Strain into a coup or martini glass, or serve on the rocks. Garnish with an apple slice and lemon peel.

Even More Appley Sidecar

This version of the sidecar adds the effervescence of cider.

1½ oz. apple brandy or calvados
¾ oz. orange liqueur
¾ oz. fresh lemon juice
3–4 oz. cider
Lemon peel and apple slice, for garnish

Shake all ingredients except cider together with ice in a shaker for 30–60 seconds. Strain into a coup or martini glass, or serve on the rocks, top with cider, stir with cocktail spoon. Garnish with an apple slice and lemon peel.

Jack Rose

This classic cocktail brings together applejack, grenadine, and lemon juice. It was quite popular in the 1920s and 1930s, and it made an appearance in Ernest Hemingway's The Sun Also Rises. *It gets its name from its blush color and the applejack in the cocktail.*

1½ oz. applejack
¾ oz. freshly squeezed lemon juice
½ oz. grenadine
Lemon peel, for garnish

Shake the applejack, lemon juice, and grenadine together in a shaker for 30–60 seconds. Strain into a chilled coup or martini glass, and garnish with a lemon peel.

Perry Old-Fashioned

You can add a little bit of cider to an old-fashioned to make it sparkle, but you can also add perry, too. And the name is just a little bit punny.

1 sugar cube
2 dashes Angostura bitters
2–3 oz. dry perry
2 oz. whiskey
Slice of pear, for garnish

Place sugar cube in the bottom of an old-fashioned or rocks glass. Dash bitters on top. Add just a drizzle of the perry, then add the whiskey. Stir until sugar is dissolved, add the remaining perry, stir, and garnish with slice of pear.

Variation: For less alcohol, just use 2 oz. more perry, and eliminate the whiskey.

Cider Apple Brandy Old-Fashioned

In Wisconsin, an old-fashioned is made more often with brandy, not whiskey, it's got muddled fruit, and it's topped with either lemon lime or sour soda. But it tastes better when it's topped with cider instead of soda, especially if it's made with apple brandy

1 sugar cube
2–3 dashes Angostura bitters
2 orange wedges
2 maraschino cherries
2 oz. apple brandy
2–3 oz. cider
Orange and maraschino cherry, for garnish

Place the sugar cube in the bottom of an old-fashioned or rocks glass. Dash the bitters on top of the cube. Then add the orange wedges and cherries, and muddle them together until the sugar is dissolved. Pour the brandy on top, and stir to combine. Add ice, top with cider, and garnish with an orange wheel or wedge and maraschino cherry.

Mitolu Cocktail
from Ramborn Hard Cider

Ramborn is a craft hard cider from Luxembourg, and the name of this cocktail comes from the origin of its ingredients: MI stands for Milan, where Campari is made; TO stands for Torino, where vermouth originates, and LU stands for Luxembourg, where Ramborn is made.

1½ oz. Campari
1½ oz. vermouth, preferably
   a fine one from Torino
3 oz. Ramborn
Orange peel, for garnish

Stir the first 3 ingredients together in a glass filled with ice, and add garnish. Enjoy, or strain into another glass without ice.

Hot Buttered Rum Cider

This aromatic and filling drink warms the belly on a cold winter's night.

1 cup boiling water (to warm mug)
2 tbsp. brown sugar
1 cinnamon stick
1 large peel of lemon or orange
3–4 whole cloves
½ tsp. vanilla extract, preferably Tahitian
6–8 oz. hard cider
2 oz. rum
2 tsp. unsalted butter

Bring 1 cup of water to a boil. In a small saucepan, place all remaining ingredients except for butter and rum, and heat to a hot simmer. Once the sugar is dissolved and mixture is starting to simmer, remove from heat, pour in rum. Pour boiling water into mug to heat mug. Once mug is thoroughly heated, discard water, add butter, then pour hot liquid on top. Enjoy.

Cider Brandy Slushie

This is a riff on a Wisconsin summer party, backyard favorite. Easy to make, and even easier to drink.

2 (12-oz.) cans frozen lemonade concentrate
6 cups water
2 cups brandy or apple brandy
Hard cider for serving

In a large bowl, whisk together lemonade concentrate, water, and brandy until smooth. Freeze overnight in a container large enough to hold all of the liquid. To serve, scoop out one or two portions the size of scoops of ice cream into a large glass, and top with about 6–8 oz. hard cider. Enjoy.

Cider Berry Rita

This drink combines the frozen fruit-flavored margarita with the effer-vescence of cider. The cider adds bubbles to the smoothie-like concoction, and together they dance on your tongue.

1½ oz. good tequila
¾ oz. orange liqueur
¾ oz. agave syrup or simple syrup
¾ oz. fresh lime juice
1 cup frozen berries, like strawberries
½ cup ice cubes
Dash citrus bitters (lime bitters are especially delicious)
3–4 oz. berry-flavored cider
Lime wheel or wedge, for garnish
Salt and sugar rim, for garnish

Pour liquors into blender, then add simple syrup, lime juice, frozen berries, ice cubes, and bitters. Blend until smooth. Rub lime around the rim of a margarita, poco, or coup glass. Pour equal amounts of sugar and salt onto a plate. Dip the glass onto the plate to coat the rim. Pour the tequila mixture into the glass, top with cider, stir once or twice, garnish with a lime wheel or wedge, and enjoy.

Sidra Margarita
From Virtue Cider
This is an even simpler twist on the margarita.

1 oz. simple syrup
2 oz. tequila or mezcal
1 oz. lime juice
Ice
2 oz. Virtue Cider
Lime wedge or wheel

Combine simple syrup, mezcal or tequila, and lime juice in a shaker with ice, and shake vigorously for about 1 minute. Strain into a glass filled with ice and top with Virtue Cider. Garnish with lime wedge or wheel.

Cider Frozé
From Virtue Cider
This is a delightfully refreshing cider cocktail for summer.

24 oz. Virtue Cider
3 oz. cherry or grapefruit juice, or any
　combination of the two
8 oz. simple syrup
Ice

Pour the cider into a large, shallow pan or ice cube tray, and freeze for at least 6 hours or until almost solid. Scrape the almost frozen cider into a blender. Add the juice, simple syrup, and 1 cup of ice. Blend until smooth, transfer the blended mixture to pitcher, and freeze until the drink has thickened, for at least 30 minutes. Blend one more time until smooth, then divide among four glasses. Enjoy.

Cider Cosmo

This is one of those drinks where cider adds a boozier and more flavorful touch to a cocktail. By using a cranberry cider, it's got just a touch of fizz, and it's a lot of fun to sip.

1½ oz. citrus vodka

1 oz. orange liqueur, like Cointreau

¼ oz. freshly squeezed lime juice

¼ oz. simple syrup

1–2 oz. cranberry cider

Lime or lemon peel twist, for garnish

Shake all ingredients, except for cider and lemon peel, in a shaker for 30–60 seconds. Add cider, stir a few times, then strain into a martini or coup glass. Garnish with a lemon or lime peel twist.

Apple Amaretto Stone Sour

A sour simply combines liquor with simple syrup and lemon or lime juice, with a ratio of usually 1½–2 oz. booze, ¾–1 oz. simple syrup, and ¾–1 oz. freshly squeezed citrus juice. A stone sour usually adds in orange juice, and often, it includes a liqueur instead of liquor. Apple and almondy amaretto go together beautifully.

1½ oz. amaretto

2 oz. freshly squeezed orange juice

½ oz. freshly squeezed lemon juice

½ oz. simple syrup

3–4 oz. cider

Orange slice and cherry, for garnish

In a shaker filled with ice, add all ingredients except cider and garnish. Shake for 30–60 seconds. Strain into a Collins or large rocks glass filled with ice. Top with cider. Wrap orange slice around cherry, slide in a toothpick, and garnish the glass. Enjoy.

Cider Mojito

This twist on a popular cocktail is even better than the original—especially if you use a flavored cider. Berry ciders, other fruit ciders, rosé ciders, and ciders with interesting flavors work especially well.

1½ oz. white or silver rum
¾ oz. mint simple syrup
¾ oz. freshly squeezed lime juice
3–4 oz. cider
Fresh mint leaves and lime, to garnish

Press a few fresh mint leaves into the bottom and sides of a tall Collins glass with a muddler—you don't actually want to muddle the mint, just press them down onto the bottom of the glass, glide them up to the top, and definitely rub the mint leaves around the rim of the glass. Discard. In a shaker filled with ice, pour rum, simple syrup, lime juice, and a few mint leaves. Shake for 30–60 seconds. Fill Collins glass with ice, pour rum mixture into glass, top with cider, then garnish with mint leaves and either a lime wedge or wheel. Stir once or twice to combine. Enjoy.

Cider Cow

Consider this a grown-up root beer float or chocolate cow. Basically, it's sparkling cider, just a touch of liqueur, pommeau, or ice cider and vanilla ice cream. Yum!

½ scoop vanilla ice cream
1 oz. liqueur, pommeau, or ice cider
4 to 6 oz. cider

Garnish: fruit related to liqueur or ice cider like raspberry if using Chambord, apple if using pommeau or ice cider

Place scoop of ice cream in the bottom of a Collins or rocks glass. Drizzle liqueur or ice cider on top, add cider, stir once or twice, and enjoy. Serve with a spoon, and garnish as desired.

Stacked Wood Cocktail

From Eden Specialty Cider

In Vermont, "Got your wood?" translates into "Are you ready for winter?" This cocktail readies you for winter, or if you're sipping it, you don't mind it so much.

I oz. Orleans Wood
I oz. bourbon
2 oz. cider
2–3 mint leaves

Pour all ingredients into a shaker with ice and mint, then shake or stir gently. Strain into a glass, garnish with a mint sprig.

Orleans Negroni

From Edens Specialty Cider

Negronis are pretty hot cocktails these days, and plenty of bars riff on them. Instead of Campari, use Orleans Bitter, along with an American vermouth.

I oz. craft gin
I oz. Orleans Bitter
I oz. American-made sweet vermouth
Orange peel

Stir all liquors together with ice until chilled, about 60 seconds. Strain into a cocktail or coupe glass, and garnish with orange peel.

Variation: To turn a negroni into a boulevardier, simply substitute the gin with bourbon.

CHAPTER 8
Food and Cider Pairings

"Yes, cider and tinned salmon are the staple diet
of the agricultural classes."
—Evelyn Waugh

IF YOU GET CIDER MAKERS and enthusiasts to talk about cider and food, your conversation could easily go on for hours. Why? Because cider pairs with food as well as—if not better than—any other alcoholic beverage. "We are biased, but we think cider is the most food-friendly beverage," says Michelle McGrath, executive director of the United States Association of Cider Makers. "And it's definitely more food-friendly than the more very hoppy beers and those really strong-bodied wines."

It naturally pairs well with lots of different foods, and it can fill in as a pairing in foods that are hard to pair with either a red or white wine. Cider naturally has more acidity than beers, and that helps with pairing foods. Its effervescence and lower alcohol content than most wines and stronger beers also add to its pairing prowess. The sugar level of many ciders can also aid in pairings, too. "Cider has got high acid, and the acid and residual sugars, depending on how dry the cider is, make really nice pairing components with food," McGrath says.

"The nice thing about pairing cider with food is that it almost sits in a place between beer and wine, allowing you to incorporate elements that make both of those beverages work so well with food," says Jason Pratt, master cicerone and senior marketing manager for MillerCoors.

Before getting into the nitty-gritty of cider and food pairing basics, the first point of order is to discuss what makes a good pairing and basic pairing principles. Then, you'll get some pairing ideas so that you can host your own cider and food pairing dinner (or meal, actually, because cider also goes well with breakfast and lunch, too!).

Pairing Basics

When food and beverage pairings are done right, both the food and the beverage will be enhanced if you taste them together. But there are two other outcomes: the beverage will overpower the food, or the food will overpower the beverage. In those two cases, instead of a perfect—or even acceptable—pairing, you're going to experience the culinary equivalent of scratching your fingernails on a chalkboard. The food tastes great by itself, the beverage tastes fine alone, but together, they do not work at all.

While this definitely happens with wine and beer—think of a stout and delicate trout pairing going awry or a white wine getting overpowered by a charcoal-grilled steak—but cider almost (though not completely) works with most foods.

The reason for this is ciders generally have less alcohol than wines, and too much alcohol can really overpower some dishes, but it's more malleable than many craft beers. "I think that cider tends to enhance the flavors in a dish rather than overwhelm them like some beers because it's lower in the tannin side than a lot of beers," says Greg Hall, owner of Virtue Cider in Michigan.

And because it often is in between red and white wines in terms of weight—alcohol content, viscosity, tannins, etc.—it pairs well with foods that both red wines and white wines pair well with, and it can fill in the gap with foods that are hard to pair with either style of wine.

Pairing Principles

There are many different thoughts when it comes to pairing food and beverages, but there are some basic ideas that you can use interchangeably when it comes to pairing ciders, wines, and beers with foods.

According to Pratt, the three things he looks for when pairing ciders (or any beverage) with food are:

Complementary flavors: "These are flavors that are similar in both the cider and the food item that really create the foundation of the pairing. Fruity elements in a dish meld with fruity elements in a cider to create a common thought-line for the pairing," he says.

Contrasting flavors: "Just like it sounds, contrasting flavors are opposites that combine to create fireworks in a pairing," he says. "When you look at the culinary world, chefs will layer contrasting flavors into the cuisine in order to bring an entire dish into balance. Things like sweet and sour are staples across a range of Asian cuisines. Salty and sweet pairings are at the core of why people love

Kansas City style barbecue sauce on smoked meat, or something as simple as caramel corn or beer and potato chips."

Cut: "This is cider's ability to cleanse the fats and oils off of your palate to ensure that each bite is as impactful as the first," Pratt says. "Because cider has alcohol, acidity, and carbonation, it is able to cut through the density of rich and fatty foods or sauces like cheese or pasta with cream based sauces."

Another pairing idea is **"goes with where it grows."** If a cuisine is specific to a region of a country where cider has traditionally been made, chances are, ciders from that region or in styles that emulate that region will go naturally with those types of foods.

Think of Normandy, France. In Normandy, the cuisine features crepes, butter, cheese (think of the creamy, bloomy rinds of Camembert or the stinky washed rinds of Pont L'Eveque), seafood, and of course, apples. All of these foods go very well with the lovely, fruit-forward *cidre* of the region.

Or think of the heavy, meat-centric food of Asturias. Asturian stew, pork shoulder, and the cave-aged, blue Cabrales cheese all sing when they're served with a natural Asturian sidra.

Another pairing principle is to either **start with the food or the beverage.** Start with one, then look for the other to match. When sommeliers and chefs work with beverage makers to design a pairings dinner, they usually start with one or the other.

That means, if you're starting with a cider, you need to understand its basic profile—is it sweet or dry? Is it tannic or acid-forward? Is it fizzy or still? What aromas do you think of when you smell this cider?

Take a cider that is flavored with some sort of herb or spice. You're going to want to incorporate rosemary into a dish that you're pairing with a rosemary cider. Or if you're working with a still, dry cider that boasts bright floral notes, you might want a dish that has a fragrance to match.

If you have a farmhouse cider made with wild apples that tastes earthy, then you'll want to go with a dish that has equal strength and perhaps even an earthy cheese to match.

But if you're starting with a dish—what are the flavor components to the dish? Is it rich and creamy? Meaty and earthy? Delicate and light? You'll want to pick a cider to match the dish.

One simple way to better pair food and cider together is **to incorporate some of the cider into the dish.** Pour the cider into the marinara while it's cooking, add it to the gravy, baste the turkey with it, add some of it into the sugar glaze for the dessert, or whisk some into the salad dressing. If you cook with the cider, the dish will naturally pair better with the cider.

The other pairing trick is to add a ***bridge*** to the dish. A bridge is a food element or ingredient that has the same flavors or aromas in the cider. For example, if you've got a cider that has grapefruit juice added or that has grapefruit aromas, you might want to create a salad with slices of grapefruit in the dish. The grapefruit will be the bridge. Or, if a cider has aromas of tropical fruits, you might want to add some tropical fruits to the dish.

When you're looking to create a perfect pairing, Pratt says that you want to combine more than one pairing element. Look to combine several pairing principles together to create a pairing that elevates both the cider and the food.

Everyone's Palate Is Different

Everyone comes to a pairing with a different palate, and there really isn't an exact science to food pairings. Sommelier and wine store owner Jaclyn Stuart says that when she used to do pairings classes for resort guests, she would often include one wine that she didn't think paired particularly well with each food item (as well as a couple of wines that did pair well). Every time, someone in that class would love that imperfect pairing, and later, Stuart would go back to taste the pairing— and she'd pick up a new note or aroma that the guest had singled out. So there isn't really a right or a wrong way to do a pairing—it's about preference.

Foods That Pair Well with Cider

Any time you start talking cider with a maker or bartender or enthusiast, two foods invariably come up: pork and cheese. Both can be considered traditional or "goes with where it grows" pairings, but they're even more important than that because they're almost fail-proof, perfect pairings. Let's start with pork.

"The message we try to get across first, with pairings, is that cider and pork always work," McGrath says. "If there's bacon, if there's ham hock, pork chops . . . cider is your beverage."

The reason for this very natural pairing is that apples simply go so well with pork. Whether it's crispy pork belly, barbecued pork shoulder, roasted pork tenderloin, sausage (all kinds: think Spanish chorizo, regular breakfast sausage, Mexican chorizo, even bratwurst), pates and charcuterie, aged hams—it doesn't matter the type of pork, pretty much each and every cider will pair with it.

This is an easy pairing, and you really don't even have to think about the style of the cider, whether it is sweet or dry. It will pair, on some level, with whatever pork dish you're serving. And if the dish contains both apples and pork, well, throw in a little bit of cider to the cooking, and the pairing will be absolutely sublime.

For example, try roasting a pork tenderloin, then creating a cider, apple, and cream sauce to go with it—it's an amazing pairing.

Cheese

If you're looking at cheese, things can get a little trickier than pork, but cheese is still a pretty natural pairing, no matter what cheese and no matter what cider you're using. "I always start with cheese," Hall says.

If you look to cheese and wine pairings as an example, the best wine, in general, for almost any kind of cheese is always a Riesling. It's usually got some sweetness—even the drier styles—but it's got nice acid, is usually fragrant or floral, and those qualities balance out the creaminess, the umami, and the saltiness of the cheese. Its acidity also cleanses the palate when you're eating cheese.

So, if you order a Riesling with your cheese plate—especially if you aren't familiar with the cheeses on the plate or there's a wide variety of cheese types on the plate—chances are, the Riesling will pair with each cheese to some degree. Some might taste better than others, but no matter what, the Riesling will pair up in some way with each cheese. We've never seen a Riesling *not* pair with cheese.

The same holds absolutely true for pretty much every cider. Ciders naturally have acidity, they naturally boast great aromas, and many of them are sweet. Not only that, but what often comes with a cheese plate? That's right: cut-up apples and/or pears. The effervescence of most ciders also cleanse the palate and lift the pairings into nirvana territory. "I really haven't seen a cider and a cheese that didn't like each other," says Eleanor Leger, founder of Virtue Cider in Vermont.

Now, just as you can get even more specific with wines—how a French sauvignon blanc goes better with a French goat cheese than a German Riesling or how Brie goes better with champagne—you can get even more detailed and persnickety with cheese and cider pairings.

Here are some specific cider styles and cheese styles to provoke your pairings:

1. Bloomy rind cheeses like Brie and Camembert go really well with French-style ciders (the "goes with where it grows" principle holds true).

2. Washed rinds, a.k.a. stinky cheeses like Taleggio and Limburger, go really well with funkier farmhouse ciders, Hall says. But the sweeter styles can also bring out the natural sweetness of these cheeses (they might smell a little strong, but they're actually pretty sweet to taste.). Leger suggests her Orleans cider apertifs also hold up well to funkier styles of cheeses. And funky Spanish cheeses go great with Spanish sidra.

3. Cheddar. "An English-style cider and an English-style cheddar—that is an absolute match made in heaven," Hall says. Leger says that Vermont cheddars go, of course, very well with Vermont ciders, too. Aged or bandage-wrapped and aged cheddars need ciders with more tannins and less sweetness, while unaged milder cheddars go better with sweeter ciders. Think how some people put cheddar cheese on their apple pies—this is the beverage equivalent.

4. Goat cheeses go well with dry, effervescent ciders and dry, still ciders with lots of aromatics. Perries also tend to go well with many goat cheeses. But, and here's an exception, if you're looking at an ash-covered, aged goat cheese, you're going to want a cider with more tannins.

5. Blue cheeses go amazingly well with ice ciders. They're an angelic partnership, with the sweetness balancing out the blue flavors, sort of like port and blue, but a different kind of beauty. Some fruit-enhanced ciders also go well with blue, just as fruit ales go well with blue cheeses.

6. Mild unaged cheeses like an unaged Gouda or Monterey Jack go well with modern, semisweet ciders—you want some sweetness, but not too much, and they match each other pretty well in weight on your palate.

7. Flavored cheeses go well with ciders that have matching flavors. A lavender honey, fresh sheep's milk cheese goes well with a lavender-enhanced sweet or semisweet cider. A chipotle-laced cheese goes well with a cider that's got some heat. And a cranberry cheddar goes well with a cranberry cider.

8. Aged non-cheddar cheeses—think Swiss or Italian aged cheeses—go very well with effervescent ciders, both sweet and dry. If the aged cheeses are a bit on the gamey or farmyard-y side, then you'll want to go with a cider that has some tannins to match them. They go really, really well with fine ciders that have a bit of a sparkle.

9. Unusual cheeses—think coffee-rubbed—go well with ciders that mimic those flavors. The lavender and coffee-rubbed cheddar-like Barely Buzzed cheese from Beehive Creamery in Utah is amazing with coffee-infused ciders like Shilling Cider's Grumpy Bear.

10. Fresh cheeses like burrata or mozzarella go very well with light, sweet, sparkling ciders.

Apple Desserts

This makes for an obvious pairing—ciders made from apples go well with apple cakes, pies, tarts, bread puddings, compotes, you name it, you'll find just about any cider will pair well with it.

Obviously, with desserts, sweeter ciders work well, but because of their origin in apples, even drier ciders can find pairing perfection. But, of course, ice ciders and apple desserts are *amazing*.

Other Desserts

For the most part, other fruits that match cider aromas—think white, light fruits like peaches, pears, apricots. They all go exceedingly well with ciders, especially ice ciders.

Red fruits—cherries, raspberries, strawberries—can sometimes work with ciders flavored with these fruits, but straight-up, unflavored ciders don't work as well.

Desserts flavored with caramel, maple, and cream also work really well with ciders, Leger says. "Anything with salted caramel is amazing," she says.

Think cheesecakes, crème brûlée, crème anglaise sauces, and bread puddings. All of these desserts also work well with ciders, especially ice ciders. And white chocolate desserts go really nicely with many ciders.

Chocolate Desserts

Like red fruit desserts, this can be a tricky pairing, and your typical cider is not going to work well. But apple brandies and some chocolate- or coffee-enhanced ciders can work with chocolate. You're going to have to experiment to find a good one. It's not an easy pairing, but it can be done.

Fried Foods

French fries, potato chips, fried pickles, fried mozzarella sticks, even fried cheesecake, all go great with almost any cider.

The reason for this is that sparkling wines go great with fried foods. So long as the cider sparkles, the fried food will sing, as the fizzing cuts through the oil and grease.

Salads

The same reason that ciders work with fried foods is the same reason they work with salads. Their fizz holds up to the vinegar in the vinaigrette.

Salads, greens-based salads anyway, can be hard to pair with wines as wines and vinegars tend to clash. But when you add a bit of sparkle, they don't clash, and instead, they fit. And since most ciders bubble, they pair really well with salads, and if you throw in a tablespoon or two of cider into the vinaigrette too, then they'll pair even more perfectly.

Creamy Dishes

The same reason cheeses work well with ciders is the reason creamy dishes work well with them—the ciders cut through the richness and fat. Alfredo sauces, cheese sauces, mashed potatoes, and anything buttery goes really well with sparkling ciders, both sweet and dry.

Red Meats

You don't usually think of ciders as pairing well with steaks, ribs, or roasts, but they really do. A lot of people pair red wines with steaks because of the tannins, but the acidity of most ciders can cut through the richness of the meat. "In Spain, they eat a ton of meat, and the high-acid ciders just cut through the meat," Hall says.

Dry ciders with good acid work really well with grilled and barbecued meats. Hall added, "I'll take acid any day for going through a nice, big piece of protein."

Medium Meats

Duck, guinea fowl, turkey, lamb, salmon or trout—all of these medium-toned flavors go really well with cider, says Leger.

A good craft cider has enough tannin to meet the weight of these meats or seafoods, but they also have enough acidity to balance it out. These foods can also be sometimes tricky to pair with either red or white wines, and cider fits right in here.

Mustard Dishes

Just as mustard goes with pork, so does cider. The apple base for ciders enhances the mustard spice, taming it and adding a touch of fragrance to the dishes. Whether it's a honey mustard chicken dish, mustard-braised greens, or even mustard whisked into a salad dressing, the cider will work.

Spicy Food and Cuisines

Anything with a lot of heat, kick, or spices tend to go well with ciders, especially sweeter ciders. Just like sweeter wines balance out the spiciness of dishes, so do sweet ciders. Think Mexican, Thai, and Indian cuisines with chilies and curry spices. The cider's sweetness and acidity balance out the heat, and together they enhance each other.

Fish and Seafood

Ciders work really well with fish and seafood, as their acidity brightens them. So long as you don't use an overly tannic cider that would overpower the fish or seafood, you will find an easy match.

Ciders also work amazingly with oysters, especially ciders with higher acid, just as sparkling wines and champagnes work well with ciders.

And mussels go great with ciders. Especially if you steam them with cider instead of beer or wine, they melt in your mouth. And in this dish, cider works better than the traditional beer or wine since the cider enhances the mussels and doesn't overpower them.

Vegetables

Just as ciders work well with salads, they also work well in pairing with other vegetable dishes. Anything au gratin or with cream sauces, or with butter or spice, ciders are going to match up nicely.

And ciders, with their acidity and sweetness, can cut through the bitterness of some vegetables. Some ciders even have some lush, vegetal notes to them so they can pair up even more perfectly.

Cider Is the Perfect Pairing Beverage for Thanksgiving

Every year around this time, wine critics, sommeliers, and other folks issue wine pairing recommendations about wine pairings for the Thanksgiving meal. And if you read these articles, there are often conflicting ideas about which wines to pair—because the meal's differing flavors are not homogenous in the least. But the most perfect beverage for this national holiday happens to be the beverage that likely was served on the original Thanksgiving tables centuries ago: cider.

The United States Association of Cider Makers and cider makers everywhere have been suggesting a radical idea: skip the wine and go with hard cider. Two years ago, they started a #pickcider campaign on social media, and folks have steadily been choosing the most American of beverages for the most American of all holidays.

"For Thanksgiving, with turkey and dressing, cider goes better than wine," says Charlotte Shelton, owner of Albemarle Ciderworks & Vintage Virginia Apples in Virginia.

The campaign started on Instagram, but it's through all media channels. Cideries throughout the country sponsor special events, suggest pairings, and offer recipes on the website, but they also increasingly are creating modern ciders and setting up special events with the holiday in mind like the cranberry cider released by Portland Cider Company annually in Portland, Oregon, or the Sasquash butternut squash, Carolina Reaper peppers, and Vermont maple syrup cider release at Bull City Ciderworks in Durham, North Carolina, or the Thanksgiving Eve Cider Release Party at Slopeswell Cider Co. in Hood River, Oregon.

"Cider's very natural at Thanksgiving," Hall says. "We're right in the heart of apple season, and we have the fresh cider coming right out of the small cider houses, sort of like a Beaujolais Nouveau of cider."

Cider is also lower in alcohol than wine, and it's higher acid than beer, and both provide better pairing options for a variety of foods. "We love wine, and we love beer, but as far as Thanksgiving dinner goes, it's a no brainer," McGrath says. "Cider pairs with a lot of things, and two of the things it pairs really well with are roasted meats and veggies, and that's what Thanksgiving is all about."

Cider naturally pairs with pork—in all of its forms, including bacon—so if that's on the table for Thanksgiving, it's a natural pairing, Shelton points out. Cider is also naturally refreshing, says Kate Ansay, operations manager for Ansay International, which imports Ramborn, the only Luxembourg-made cider to the United States. "Cider cuts the heaviness of the turkey, gravy, and mashed potatoes," Ansay says.

"It's also more sessionable," says Chandra Rudolph, owner of the Lost Valley cider bar and a cider maker in Milwaukee, Wisconsin. "You want to be able to enjoy Thanksgiving. And who doesn't have apples on their Thanksgiving table?"

Apple pies, apples in stuffing, apples with cheese on the appetizer platter or mixed in a vegetable dish . . . it's a natural pairing. But don't get hung up on pairing them at the Thanksgiving table, McGrath cautions. "A good pairing is not necessarily about matching apple cider with apple pie, but it's also about contrasting flavors," McGrath says. "For example, Cider Craft magazine recommended choosing a sour cider to pair with sweet potatoes, a contrasting experience."

McGrath says some people decide to buy three or four different ciders to aim for perfectly pairing several dishes on your Thanksgiving table. "But a dry, sparkling, heritage cider is going to be pleasing with everything on your table," McGrath adds.

Cooking with Cider

Anytime you add the beverage to the dish you want to pair it with, the pairing will work better. Cooking with cider is a wonderful experience, and it can enhance everything from gravies to vinaigrettes to desserts to cheese sauces. A good rule of thumb is that if you can cook the dish with beer or wine added, you can use cider instead. Here are some ideas for experimenting in your kitchen with cider:

Cheese Dishes

Fondue is amazing with cider. So is a ¼ cup or ½ cup of cider added to a sauce for mac 'n cheese or au gratin potatoes. And a welsh rarebit sandwich works so well with an English cider. But one word of wisdom: don't use a rosé or flavored cider, as the cheese sauce will turn out pink!

Sauces

Gravies, basting meats, reductions, and even spaghetti sauces can all be enhanced with ciders. Cream sauces, beurre blancs, and anything that uses wine or vinegar reductions can use cider instead. You can even pour a little bit of cider into your apple stuffing for thanksgiving, and you can also toss some into your chili or beef stew, too.

Pork Dishes

Pour some cider into your barbecue sauce, add it to your pork tenderloin, put it in your rillette, or braise your sausages in it. Cider, of course, will make your pork dishes sing.

Mustard

If your recipe calls for mustard, add a tablespoon or two of cider. It works, and it works well.

Marinades

Any marinade you make with beer or wine can be made with cider. Whether you're marinating pork chops, steaks, or chicken breasts, cider adds flavor and oomph.

Poaching

If you're going to steam mussels or poach fish, use cider instead of wine or beer. You can also poach chicken in it, too.

Salad Dressings

Vinaigrettes can be enhanced with cider, but so can creamy ranch dressings. Just a little goes a long way in salad dressings, though.

Desserts

Obviously, any apple pies, tarte tatins, compotes, and bread puddings can be enhanced with cider, pommeau, or ice ciders.

Crème anglaise, caramel desserts, and creamy desserts also are enhanced with a little bit of cider or ice cider. In fact, a very simple dessert is to simply take vanilla, caramel, or other non-chocolate ice cream and top it with just a drizzle of ice cider or pommeau.

And baked desserts like cakes can also be enhanced with cider. Instead of a rum cake, use apple brandy or ice cider for a decadent, apple twist.

APPENDIX
Cider Definitions

ABV: Alcohol by Volume.

Aperitifs: also known as aperitivos, these are traditionally European (usually in France or Italy) bitter liqueurs that are wine or spirit-based products, flavored with citrus, herbs, spices and roots.

Apple brandy: brandy made from apples, not grapes. Sometimes known as calvados.

Apple essence: sometimes called fruit essence or a by-product from making apple concentrate that has the aromas and flavors of apples, which have, in a sense, been extracted out in the process of making apple juice concentrate.

Apple juice concentrate: also known as apple concentrate, a highly processed form of juice.

Apple wine: a fermented beverage from the juice of apples that has a higher content of alcohol than hard cider and is often produced in a slightly different way than hard cider. But, the term is almost interchangeable with hard cider.

Applejack: once referred to American apple brandy, but now refers to a blend of at least 20 percent apple distillate with a neutral grain spirit that's then aged for at least four years in used bourbon barrels.

Autosiphon: basically a pump or a piece of equipment that moves your cider from one container to another with ease.

Backsweetening: adding sugar (brown, white, turbinado, etc.), corn sugar (dextrose), honey, molasses, maple syrup, or any other sugar to increase the sweetness level of a cider after fermentation has stopped.

Brewing: the first step, after steeping, for making beer. Cider is never brewed, while beer always is brewed (before it is fermented).

Bridge: a food element or ingredient that has the same flavors or aromas in the beverage you are pairing the food with.

Calvados: apple brandy made under strict control in France.

Campden tablet: sodium metabisulfate is used to control yeast and stop fermentation.

Carboy: a plastic or glass container that's used to ferment wine, cider, mead, or beer. It is sometimes called a demijohn.

Chapitalization: a winemaking technique also used in cider making in which sugar is added before fermentation.

Cicerone: the certification for beer what a master sommelier is to wine. It is a certified designation, and cicerones have to pass rigorous exams to attain the designation.

Cider: unfermented apple juice, in the United States. Also, see *Sweet Cider.*

Cider apples: apples used in making of hard cider, come in four categories of sweets, bittersweets, sharps and bittersharps. Except for sweets, not usually good eating apples.

Cider beer: not a real thing, but what people sometimes call hard cider because they think it is in the same genre of alcohol as beer.

Culinary apples: also known as dessert apples, used primarily for eating purposes, but also used in both craft and commercial cider making.

Demijohn: see Carboy.

Dessert apples: see culinary apples.

Fermentation: the process in which yeast converts sugar in a beverage to alcohol.

Fermentation lock: also sometimes called an *airlock*, is a piece of equipment that fits on the top of a carboy or a glass jug that keeps bacteria and other bad stuff out the cider you're fermenting, but it also allows the carbon dioxide gas, produced by the yeasts, to escape without exploding.

Finish: the lingering flavors, aromas, and sensations you feel after you drink a cider.

Hard cider: fermented apple juice or beverage made from fermented apples, apple juice or apple juice concentrate.

Hydrometer: a cylindrical piece of equipment that measures the density of a liquid. In cider making, you use this to measure the alcohol content of the cider.

Malic acid: naturally occurring acid in apples, can be added to a cider that tastes watery or unbalanced after fermentation.

Mashing: the process in making beer in which grains are soaked in hot water.

Mouthfeel: the sensation of what an alcoholic beverage feels like in your mouth; it is both the texture and the weight of the beverage.

Oxidizer: a type of alkali cleaner you use *before* you sanitize your equipment.

Perry: sometimes referred to as pear cider, as perry is basically hard cider made from pears, not apples. Some ciders contain juice from both apples and pears, and those can rightfully be called pear ciders.

Polyphenols: the chemical compounds in cider, wine, and beer that affect the taste, aromas, and mouthfeel; also, many of them have health benefits.

Pomace: the fruity leftovers from pressing cider or wine.

Sanitizer: food-grade sanitizer is a must for keeping your cider equipment free from contamination.

Shrub: a traditional vinegar, fruit, and sugar beverage; can be enjoyed straight, diluted with water or seltzer, or combined into cocktails.

Simple syrup: a water and sugar syrup used to sweeten cocktails, usually equal parts sugar and water or sometimes more sugar than water.

Still: an alcoholic beverage—usually a wine or a cider—that has no effervescence or bubbles.

Sweet cider: pasteurized apple juice. Apple growers added the "sweet" modifying adjective in the 1800s to denote its difference from what was simply known as cider or what is known today as hard cider.

Tannins: the chemical compounds found in fruits (often the skins and seeds) that create a bitter or dry or chalky or puckered feeling in your mouth.

Varietal cider: a cider made from a single type of apple. These apples sometimes are known as vintage apples.

Vinifera grapes: the species of grapes that get made into wine; *Vitis vinifera* is a separate species of grapes from table grapes; vinifera grapes have thicker skins and are juicier than table grapes, making them better suited for wine production.

Wine thief: a plastic or glass piece of equipment that allows you to remove samples of fermenting cider from a jug or carboy.

Wort: after a beer mash is created, the result is called wort, which then gets brewed with hops and/or spices before being fermented with yeast to create beer.

Acknowledgments

The author would like to thank all of the cider makers, bartenders, bar owners, and cider experts who shared their time and expertise with her, especially: Greg Hall, Eleanor Leger, Kate Ansay, Robert Purman, Mattie Beason, Ambrosia Borowski, Jessica Shabatura, Walker Fanning, Eric West, Michelle McGrath, Paul Vander Heide, Stephanie Zipp, Charlotte Shelton, Jason Pratt, Jaclyn Stuart, John Enzenauer, Chandra Rudolph, Rob Ebert, Tom Donda, Patricia Wood, Jennifer O'Flanagan, and Lior Vainer. She would also like to thank her editor Leah Zarra and her agent Marilyn Allen.

About the Author

Jeanette Hurt first discovered cider, er, *sidra*, when she was a college student living in Madrid. Her roommate Beth introduced her to cider, and she's been seeking out good ciders ever since. She's the author of a dozen books, including the critically acclaimed *Drink Like a Woman*, and she covers "the indulgence of all things distilled, brewed, and fermented" for *Forbes*. In real life, when she's not sipping a fine cider or shaking a cocktail at her backyard tiki bar, you can often find her walking along the shore of Lake Michigan with her husband, their son, and their Chihuahua-Great Pyrenees mix. You can find her on Twitter or Instagram at @byJeanetteHurt.

Index

Conversion Charts

Metric and Imperial Conversions

(These conversions are rounded for convenience)

Ingredient	Cups/ Tablespoons/ Teaspoons	Ounces	Grams/ Milliliters
Fruit, dried	1 cup	4 ounces	120 grams
Fruits or veggies, chopped	1 cup	5 to 7 ounces	145 to 200 grams
Fruits or veggies, puréed	1 cup	8.5 ounces	245 grams
Honey, maple syrup, or corn syrup	1 tablespoon	0.75 ounce	20 grams
Liquids: cream, milk, water, or juice	1 cup	8 fluid ounces	240 milliliters
Salt	1 teaspoon	0.2 ounces	6 grams
Spices: cinnamon, cloves, ginger, or nutmeg (ground)	1 teaspoon	0.2 ounce	5 milliliters
Sugar, brown, firmly packed	1 cup	7 ounces	200 grams
Sugar, white	1 cup/ 1 tablespoon	7 ounces/0.5 ounce	200 grams/12.5 grams
Vanilla extract	1 teaspoon	0.2 ounce	4 grams

Liquids

8 fluid ounces = 1 cup = ½ pint

16 fluid ounces = 2 cups = 1 pint

32 fluid ounces = 4 cups = 1 quart

128 fluid ounces = 16 cups = 1 gallon